the **NO-NONSENSE** guide to

TERRORISM

Jonathan Barker

'Publishers have created lists of short books that discuss the questions that your average [electoral] candidate will only ever touch if armed with a slogan and a soundbite. Together [such books] hint at a resurgence of the grand educational tradition... Closest to the hot headline issues are *The No-Nonsense Guides*. These target those topics that a large army of voters care about, but that politicos evade. Arguments, figures and documents combine to prove that good journalism is far too important to be left to (most) journalists.'

Boyd Tonkin,
The Independent,
London

The No-Nonsense Guide to Terrorism
First published in the UK by
New Internationalist™ Publications Ltd
Oxford OX4 1BW, UK
www.newint.org
New Internationalist is a registered trade mark.

in association with
Verso
6 Meard Street
London
W1F 0EG
www.versobooks.com

Cover image: Alan Hughes

Design by New Internationalist Publications Ltd.
Series editor: Troth Wells

Printed by TJ International Ltd, Padstow, Cornwall, UK.

British Library Cataloguing-in-Publication Data.
A catalogue record for this book is available from the British Library.

Library of Congress Cataloguing-in-Publication Data.
A catalogue for this book is available from the Library of Congress.

ISBN 1-85984-433-2

the **NO-NONSENSE** guide to
TERRORISM
Jonathan Barker

About the author
Jonathan Barker lives in Toronto where he works as writer and researcher. He taught political science at the University of Toronto for many years. He has also taught at the University of Dar es Salaam and the University of Arizona. He has done research on local politics in Senegal, Tanzania, India and Uganda. His books include *Street-Level Democracy: Political Settings at the Margins of Global Power* (Toronto: Between the Lines and West Hartford, Connecticut: Kumarian, 1999) and *Rural Communities under Stress: Peasant Farmers and the State in Africa* (Cambridge: Cambridge University Press, 1989).

Acknowledgements
Jorge Nef and Richard Swift helped the ideas to fit together and match the subject matter. Gillian Barker, Nick Thompson and Penny Thompson helped to get the words to match the ideas. Troth Wells made useful suggestions and kept the process rolling. Nancy Barker cleared the decks and refreshed the mind.

Foreword

IN A WORLD that is fraught with crisis and in which transnational and cultural divisions are hardening, Jonathan Barker's wide-ranging yet remarkably succinct *No-Nonsense Guide to Terrorism* is an extraordinarily timely aid to making sense of the complex and often violent responses to the attacks on New York and Washington.

Since those atrocities of 11 September, a 'war on terror' has unfolded across the world. Direct action by US forces or their associates has involved a full-scale war in Afghanistan, action in Yemen, Pakistan, Georgia and the Philippines, support for counter-insurgency forces in many countries, and a hardening of legal instruments of control that is almost global in its extent.

There is little evidence that it is working, but this seems to make no difference to the persistent efforts now being made. The al-Qaeda network and its many associates remain active, and grass-roots support for them may even be increasing.

The US is increasing its military spending back towards peak Cold-War levels and has brought in an openly-acknowledged policy of violent pre-emption against movements or states that are seen as enemies. Some states – Iran, Iraq, North Korea, Syria, Libya and Cuba – are even seen as greater or lesser participants in a veritable 'axis of evil', determined to combat a morally certain US as it readily assumes leadership of a movement towards a global civilization rooted in the free market.

Some see the war on terror as an act of desperation, others argue cogently that it relates to an utter determination to regain control of a fractured global system in which the innate vulnerabilities of an advanced state were demonstrated by the attacks in New York and Washington.

Whatever the reality, a common theme is a steadfast concern with defeating terrorist groups, coupled with a persistent lack of concern with the underlying motivations of the groups and the contexts within which they draw their considerable support. Nor is much attention given to the much greater and more persistent problem of state terrorism – a mode of extreme political violence that has cost millions rather than thousands of lives in the past half century.

Jonathan Barker's analysis in this book is remarkable in several respects. It places the events of the past couple of years in a much wider context, ranging widely over the problems of terrorism of recent decades. It brings together precise descriptions and sharp analysis of the many instances of state terrorism, rightly pointing to the frequent involvement of western states.

Furthermore, it shows how terrorism and its response constrain democratic political discussion and action. Political rights and liberties are restricted and a moralistic language is employed that can even mirror that of the terrorist.

Most significantly, this book puts the atrocities of 11 September, and the subsequent military responses, in the context of a divided world in which the increasing socio-economic divisions are leading to a degree of bitterness and alienation that is rarely recognised in western states.

This book is an excellent contribution to our understanding of the issues and deserves a very wide readership. In particular, it should be required reading for any western security analyst, policy adviser or politician concerned in any way with responding to the events of 11 September 2001.

Paul Rogers
Professor of Peace Studies
Bradford University, UK

the **NO-NONSENSE** guide to
TERRORISM

CONTENTS

the NO-NONSENSE guide to

TERRORISM

TERRORISM CAME AND found me, forced me to
write about it. Most of my writing has focused on local
political action. What impedes it? What makes it work?
But after the airplanes plunged into the World Trade
Center and the Pentagon, I found myself spending
long hours each day reading compulsively about terrorism. One of my daughters lives in Brooklyn so
family concerns were part of my reaction. It took a
while for horrified disbelief to leave room for questions. But questions came. Where did the will to
terrorism come from? Had I been ignoring a real and
growing danger? Was Bush's War on Terrorism infect-
ing politics everywhere with the virus of Good vs Evil?
Was the political Right fated to gain unity and strength
from fighting terrorism? Were the Left and Center
Left bound to be driven to paralysis and division?

The terrorists forced to my attention an aspect of
politics I have preferred to ignore. Violence and intimidation, I had figured, are always an ugly presence. But
their very universality made it safe to set them aside.
Now it seemed they were driving the train. It was time
to take a long look at the ugly side. An immediate
problem was cynicism. Could any official statement or
main-stream news item be taken at face value?
Conspiracy theories could hardly be ignored since terrorism, including state terrorism, always involves
deception and hidden agents. I decided to be careful
and skeptical, but to leave the pursuit of conspiracy to
experts. I could already see some consequences of terrorism. Conspiracy talk pulled talented analysts away
from other important political issues and it called into

question the credibility of all political speech. From the outset terrorism and the response to it diverts and devalues politics.

The topic presented other difficulties. News stories, at their best, dig into the lives and actions of terrorists and the workings of their networks and cells. The reporting is often courageous and useful. But, with my skepticism aroused, I had to recall that governments shape and even manufacture news about terrorism and that terrorist organizations, too, create news coverage that will further their aims. When I turned to the magazines I rely upon to see my way through complex issues, I was amazed at how quickly commentators found in the rubble of the WTC corroboration of their long-held positions. Fresh insights were infrequent. Part of my task became understanding how ideologies and interests use terrorism to shape public thinking.

The walk on the ugly side is fraught with emotion. The expression of hatred in politics has reached depths not seen since red scare times. Possibly since the Second World War. The hatreds attached to terrorism and counter-terrorism have local and popular existence in religious commitments and cultural identities all over the world. Expression of hatred is so common that a good portion of political speech gets devoted to clarifying exactly who one hates. Signaling hatred poisons the well of mutual recognition that waters political dialogue and accommodation.

On terrorism I try not to be dismissive of anyone's ideas, but to evaluate them on their merits. We need clear understanding of the dangers of terrorism and counter-terrorism to assure security and freedom ñ and to defend and enlarge the ability of people everywhere to work together democratically to resolve the problems that loom largest in their lives.

Jonathan Barker
Toronto

1 Questioning terrorism

The attacks of 11 September 2001 on the World Trade Center and the Pentagon with their haunting images of falling people and collapsing skyscrapers generated great passion and raised large questions. Careful analysis, while acknowledging the emotional impact of terrorism, must still look with clear eyes on the sources and consequences of terrorist acts and the measures taken in response.

BEFORE THE PERFECTION of dynamite by Alfred Nobel in the 1860s it was difficult to kill people indiscriminately and in large numbers. In the 1790s it took the resources of Robespierre's Jacobin government in revolutionary France to round up hundreds of thousands of suspects and turn the guillotine, with its official toll of 17,000 executions, into the symbol and the instrument of the Reign of Terror. The conservative British politician, Edmund Burke, was among the first to use the terms 'terrorism' and 'terrorist'. He wanted to draw attention to the murderous excesses of the Jacobin state and its 'strong corp of irregulars... let loose on the people', a perfect example of state terrorism using proxies. In the late 1800s Russian anarchists adopted the terms, describing proudly as 'terrorism' the stabbing, strangling or shooting of selected state officials. Since then few have claimed the labels; they have been reserved as terms of abuse to describe one's enemies.

For clarity I will use the term 'group terrorism' for the terrorist acts of non-state groups and 'state terrorism' for similar actions undertaken by governments. Both are important parts of this story. For some purposes finer distinctions of kinds of terrorism are necessary: anti-colonial nationalist, right-wing, left-wing, anarchist, nationalist, religious, internal state, external state, colonial, state terrorism by proxy, and more.

A few brief accounts illustrate varieties of terrorist incidents that have long been familiar to modern politics.

1 Suicide bombing: *Before he left the village that night, 24-year-old Nabil sorted out a few things. At four in the afternoon he went to see his cousin Abdullah Halabiyeh, who lived next door, and paid him back the $15 he had owed him for a year and a half. Then he cleaned his new car for nearly two hours. At 6 pm, he handed over a petition he had been gathering to get the local council to tar the road outside the family home and told Abdullah to keep hassling them until the job was done. And then at 9.30 pm he went to his bare room to pray.*

'He was crying and saying Qur'an. After 10 minutes or nearly 15 he finished the prayer. And I asked him [why he was] making a long time in the praying and he said nothing and smiled,' Abdullah said.

Abdullah watched him drive off around 10 pm. Nabil's final destination was only 10 minutes away so he must have stopped somewhere to pick up his companion and fellow villager Osama Bahar, and the explosives they would wrap round their waists. At about 11.30 pm they walked into Jerusalem's crowded Ben Yehuda pedestrian shopping mall and, in the midst of the bright lights and chatting teenagers, pulled the detonators. Nails and shrapnel, mixed in with the explosives, mutilated anyone within 20 feet of these two exploding human bombs. Eleven Israelis were killed and 37 injured. There was little of the bombers left to pick up…[1]

2 Disappearance: *On 27 January 1977 Dagmar Hagelin, then 17 years old, traveled across Buenos Aires, Argentina to visit her friend, Norma Burgos. But Norma had been arrested the previous day. In her apartment seven military men lay in ambush. Led by Alfredo Astiz, a young naval officer and agent in the military regime's 'dirty war' against its leftist opponents, they were hoping to nab other subversives. When Astiz tried to grab Dagmar, she turned and ran. Alfredo and another soldier gave chase. When Dagmar stretched her lead* *to about 100 feet (30 meters) Alfredo knelt, took aim with his regulation pistol and with a single shot brought her down. The soldiers commandeered a taxi at gunpoint, put the bleeding girl in the trunk and sped away. She was never seen again.*[2]

3 *Targeted assassination*: *On the morning of 8 June 2000 in Athens, Greece, Heather Saunders waved good-bye to her husband, the British defense attaché Brigadier Stephen Saunders, as he headed to work. When Mr Saunders stopped his car at a set of traffic lights opposite the Olympic Stadium, two men on a moped pulled alongside and one fired four shots through the passenger window. Mr Saunders died on his way to hospital.*[3]

4 *Targeted state terror*: *On 19 May 1994 in San Salvador someone broke into the offices shared by the Salvadoran Women's Movement (MSM) and the Madeleine Lagadec Human Rights Center. The following day unidentified gunmen killed Alexander Rodas Abarca as he was guarding the offices. He was a reserve member of the National Police and member of the security group for the Farabundo Marti National Liberation Front (FMLN), a guerrilla movement that became a political party under the terms of the 1992 peace accords. The directors of the two organizations said that the staff of the office had seen people and vehicles watching the premises for some days before the incident.*[4]

These are acts chilling in their familiarity but they illustrate important differences. Suicide bombers aim to kill and maim dozens among the broad cross-section of people in a public mall. Other killers select narrower targets. The moped assassins choose a foreign military official. The state terrorists go after activist youths in one case and human rights workers in another. In one case they keep the state connection obscure.

Shootings and bombings have become familiar occurrences in many countries, but they are not the only terrorist acts. In the 1980s airplane hijackings, often by persons claiming to have automatic weapons or bombs in their possession, became a frequent technique in the terrorist repertoire. The hijackers would take passengers hostage and bargain with authorities for one or more of several things: money, safe passage to a friendly country, the release of comrades, or publicity about their cause. Sometimes airplanes were sabotaged with bombs hidden on board, timed to destroy the craft in the air and kill both passengers and crew. Terrorists also used massive car and truck bombs hooked to timers or to remote controls, to kill people and to damage buildings of symbolic importance like the US Marine Barracks in Beirut in 1983, the Grand Hotel in Brighton in 1984 during the Tory Party Conference or the Murrah Federal Building in Oklahoma City in 1995.

Upping the ante

Like suicide bombers, the men who crashed passenger jets into the WTC and Pentagon were determined to die with their victims, but added a new wrinkle by employing hijacked airplanes with their loads of volatile fuel as giant exploding missiles. The combination was original. So was the scale of the operation with intricate planning to deploy four carefully organized teams. The suicide attackers were also unusual for their mature age and their professional credentials, as well as the special training undertaken by those assigned to pilot the hijacked aircraft into their high profile and densely populated targets. The targets stood as symbols of the global economic and military power of the US. Al-Qaeda, a loosely organized transnational network, seemed to be the instigator of the attacks. It aims to challenge and weaken the global power of the US and to drive US influence from the holy places of Islam.

There is an ongoing debate about whether world history has entered a new phase since 11 September

2001. There is no doubt, however, that terrorism and counter-terrorism have entered a new era. The biggest fear is that terrorists will break the barrier imposed by ordinary explosives and find a way to deploy nuclear, biological or chemical (NBC) weapons. The *Aum Shinrikyo* sect in Japan made the technical break with its Sarin gas attack in the Tokyo subway in 1995, but their method of dispersing the poison was defective and they killed 12 people instead of the thousands they had intended.

September 11 2001

The attacks in New York and Washington demonstrated that older methods artfully combined could do tremendous damage: more than 3,000 victims, two enormous towers of the World Trade Center and the people inside smashed into dust and debris. Add to that major damage to the Pentagon, the heart of US military planning. In one spectacular operation al-Qaeda demolished the architectural symbol of the global economic power of the US and damaged the

Six months of terrorism (from July to December 1996)

June 25: Islamic radical terrorists opposed to the Western military presence in the Gulf region, explode a truck bomb next to a US Air Force housing area at Dhahran, Saudi Arabia, killing 19 American service personnel and injuring 385 more.

July 17: Tamil Tiger guerillas explode a train bomb killing 70 and injuring 600 people in Sri Lanka after Government troops mounted a successful offensive on the east of the island.

August 3: One person killed and 111 people injured in small bomb explosion in Centennial Square during Atlanta Olympics Games.

August 26: Six Iraqi dissidents hijack a Sudan Airways A310 Airbus en route from Khartoum to Jordan and divert it to Stansted, England. After eight and one-half hours negotiating with British authorities the hijackers release all the 13 crew and 180 passengers unharmed.

October 7: IRA terrorists penetrate security at the British Army's Northern Ireland Headquarters at Lisburn, south of Belfast, to plant two car bombs. One soldier is killed in the blasts and 30 other people injured.

SIPRI Yearbook 2001, Stockholm International Peace Research Institute, June 2001.

icon of its military might. The mesmerizing images of the big Boeings flying through the outer walls of New York's WTC towers and these colossal structures collapsing downward into themselves captured a global audience. But emotions and questions that the images awakened are far from uniform. Americans felt an overwhelming mixture of horror, fear, sorrow and anger. This was shared widely in other countries. Almost everyone sympathized with the victims and their families, but beyond that the response to the symbolism of the attacks was more diverse.

People who recorded their reactions in the web space provided by the British Broadcasting Corporation in the aftermath of September 11 unanimously deplored the terrorist actions. Some called for immediate retribution against the perpetrators and their supporters. A few expressed fear of their own anger and desire for revenge. Several wanted to know what the US had done to be so hated. Others could think of Western actions that might well motivate terrorist attacks. The French newspaper of the moderate

December 20: IRA terrorists try to kill Unionist politician in a Belfast hospital, injuring a policeman. The attack sparks a series of bomb, mortar and rocket attacks on the security forces that continue on a daily basis into January. Protestant terrorists also stage car bomb attacks on republicans.

December 23: Corsican militants explode a bomb at the French national statistics office in Paris causing no casualties. A car bomb in the Algerian capital, Algiers, kills three and injures 70 people in cafe near the port. Islamic GIA guerrillas are blamed.

December 24: Four people killed by pipe bomb in supermarket in Worcester, near Cape Town, South Africa, and dozens injured in the blast, which was attributed to white extremists of the Afrikaaner Resistance Movement (AWB).

December 25: Tibetan activists explode bomb in Lhasa, Tibet, near government offices in protest at Chinese rule, injuring five people.

December 31: Sixty people killed when train is blown up by a bomb in Sensapani, Assam, India, by tribal guerrillas. ■

Terrorism Programme, Centre for Defence and International Security Studies, Lancaster University left, *Le Monde*, splashed the headline 'We are all Americans', sparking a lively flow of letters from readers, many of whom identified as much with the afflicted and injured in the global South as with the anguished and bereaved in New York and Washington.

No government expressed support for the assaults, while many countries expressed sympathy and support. A variety of Muslim leaders spoke of their sadness and horror. Unofficial responses were more varied. Many spoke of their shock, grief and fear. Orphan Pamuk, the Turkish writer, saw a woman weeping openly on the street in Istanbul. He also noticed the 'detached amazement' with which patrons of a coffee shop in Istanbul watched the television images. He observed that people would often follow their denunciation of the 'despicable... slaughter of innocent people' with criticism of the 'political and economic power' of the US. One old working man confided to him, 'Sir, have you seen, they have bombed America. They did the right thing.' But after seeing images of the carnage he regretted his remark.[5] There were reports of impromptu celebrations in Nablus and East Jerusalem, and in Arab neighborhoods of Ciudad del Este, Paraguay.

The French social thinker Jean Baudrillard created a stir among intellectuals when he claimed in an article in *Le Monde* that the symbolism of the collapsing towers resonates deeply in the minds of Westerners: 'This terrorist imagination... unconsciously inhabits us all. We have dreamed of this event... everybody without exception has dreamed of it, because nobody can fail to dream of the destruction of any power that has become hegemonic to that degree.'[6]

President George W Bush, in his speech to Congress on 20 September, proclaimed 'a war on terror' that 'begins with al-Qaeda, but... will not end until every terrorist group of global reach has been found, stopped and defeated.' 'And,' he added, 'we will pursue nations that provide aid or safe haven to terrorism.

Every nation, in every region, now has a decision to make. Either you are with us, or you are with the terrorists.' A long list of countries declared support and the polls showed the President had the overwhelming backing of the US public.[7]

The new focus on terrorism spread rapidly. Other governments and officials also found it politically useful to adopt anti-terrorist stances that ruled certain groups and certain ideas beyond the bounds of political dialogue. Israeli spokespersons were quick to treat the Palestinian Liberation Organization (PLO) and Yasser Arafat, President of the Palestinian Authority, as terrorists on the same footing as extremist Hamas and Hizbullah. Arafat denied that the PLO was a terrorist organization and President Bashar al-Assad of Syria lectured UK Prime Minister Tony Blair about the difference between the state terrorism visited by Israel on the Palestinians and the necessarily violent resistance undertaken by Palestinian freedom fighters.

Reaction elsewhere

Further afield, President Mugabe of Zimbabwe applied the label terrorism to the movement opposing his authoritarian rule and to journalists who reported this resistance. He then set about using stringent police measures against them. President Sukarnoputri of Indonesia at first protested that her country should be on the US Government's list of those afflicted by al-Qaeda terrorism because of the fighting in Sulawesi. Then her government refused to accept the US view that an active Muslim association, Jemaah Islamiah, was linked to al-Qaeda. The bombing of a nightclub in Bali on 12 October 2002, killing almost 200 people, and the subsequent arrest of some of the alleged perpetrators convinced the Indonesians that the US view had merit.

Reactions hostile to the US became much more common and overt after the US began bombing Afghanistan, although even then the popular demonstrations in Pakistan, Egypt, Indonesia and other countries were not nearly as large or ferocious as predicted. Voices of criticism within the US and its close supporters also grew louder, although they were scantily reported in the main television news programs and newspapers. Noam Chomsky, professor of linguistics and longtime critic of US state terrorism, published a scathing study that cited US involvement in terrorism as one of the causes of anti-American sentiment of groups like al-Qaeda and condemned the war on Afghanistan as neither reasonable nor effective as a response to the attacks.[8]

Without the benefit of advertising or major reviews, Chomsky's book became an instant bestseller. Other critics argued their views on several different grounds: principled nonviolence, the judgment that military operations were only recruiting more anti-Western terrorists, and a belief that diplomacy and intelligence were a better way to capture terrorists, Some even held the idea that the US Government had manipulated the event in order to strengthen its position in central Asia ensuring access to the oil reserves in the basin of the Caspian sea.

An American professor was startled to discover in his seminars on democracy held in South Africa (January 2002) and Poland (July 2002) that the threat most feared by participants was not terrorism and the danger posed by al-Qaeda. These committed activists from all over the world were more worried about the implications of the US war on terrorism. They were especially apprehensive about the increased power it gave to the security services of their home governments to block the democratic activities they were working to promote. One participant raised the troubling idea that in order to defend democracy at home the US was systematically wrecking democratic forces elsewhere.[9]

The attack on the symbols of global economic and military power in the US was probably much more successful than even the terrorists could have hoped.

The video tape with an elated Osama bin Laden praising the martyr-militants suggests that even he was surprised with the WTC collapse and the extent of the destruction. Other bin Laden tapes were prime-time news in the Middle East and elsewhere in the Muslim world where at least part of the audience heard with satisfaction his denunciations of the West and the corrupt Middle East governments that allowed US soldiers on holy land and defiled the Islamic faith. Western commentators began worrying about which side was winning the sympathy of 'the Arab street'.

Emotions and standpoints

The first thing to confront in writing or reading about terrorism is so obvious that it often escapes mention, yet it stands as one of the obstacles to clear thinking, adequate discussion and good analysis. One has to think about ugly events, horrifying actions that kill and injure unsuspecting people going about their daily lives. One has to focus on the terrible effects of deaths, injuries and destruction on those whose worlds and bodies are torn to pieces by explosions designed to kill, maim and frighten. One has to reflect on the people who undertake such unthinkable actions, on those who design and plan atrocities actually hoping for deadly results. Like the victims, like the survivors and like us, these terrorists are human beings. The questions are unavoidable: what makes us capable of such acts? Are there conditions under which I might do something similar? Reflecting on terrorist acts is the stuff of blame and tears, raised voices and raised fists, sleeplessness and nightmares.

That such acts arouse strong emotions is no accident. A core purpose of 'propaganda by the deed' dating from the 19th century anarchists has been to sway the minds and emotions of people. Some commentators and lay people find terrorism so repugnant that they reject the search for reasons for its occurrence. Consider these remarks by Marcus Gee, a journalist specializing in international politics at Toronto's *Globe and Mail*:

> [T]he roots of September 11 lie in hatred (anti-Americanism) and ideology (radical Islam). To say otherwise – to say that the terrorists were driven to do what they did because of political or social conditions... is to absolve them of moral responsibility for what they did... When you condemn American misdeeds in the same breath as condemning September 11, you draw a parallel – a moral equivalence... that lends legitimacy to the terrorists... I'll tell you why that's dangerous: because it incites hatred against Americans. There's a direct line between the irrational anti-Americanism that is rife in so many parts of the world and the attacks of September 11. Have you noticed that many of the things bin Laden and his ilk criticize about the United States – its supposed arrogance, its soulless materialism, its junk culture, its predatory capitalism – are echoed almost to the word by its critics in the West.

This call for the silencing of voices and the shunning of analysis is precisely the reaction that stands in the way of clear thinking and useful dialogue about terrorism. Marcus Gee is right, however, to emphasize the strong emotions and the drive for moral justification that terrorist acts arouse. In order to communicate we must acknowledge these responses in ourselves and in others.

Precisely because it engages our deepest feelings and challenges our moral commitments, terrorism takes on a political potency rivaled only by war and by deep-seated ideological or religious differences. Terrorism is often associated with war or fear of war and with ideological positioning, so political agendas bristle forth in most communication on the subject. Recognizing the emotional force of the topic, experts often try to burnish feelings of righteousness rather than strive to enlighten understanding and challenge prejudice. They use the words 'terrorism' and 'terrorist' to denote the actions, ideas, people and organizations that, from their standpoint, lie beyond the boundaries of reason, ethics and interest that govern ordinary politics. A writer for a publication of the Hoover Institution, a conservative think-tank with many connections to President Bush's inner circle, praises the President for identifying the targets of the US as 'the evil ones'. He explains, 'our enemy has already dehumanized himself... You do not try to appease them, or persuade them, or reason with them. You try, on the contrary, to outwit them, to vanquish them, to kill them. You behave with them in the same manner that you would deal with a fatal epidemic – you try to wipe it out.'[10]

The words 'terrorism' and 'terrorist' are themselves pejorative. Nowhere is the political loading more evident than in the refusal of governments to recognize their own terrorist actions. Those who speak for governmental authority speak with conviction about fighting the evil of terrorism. They enumerate the death and damage perpetrated by terrorist bombs while holding silence about the death and damage to civilians and bystanders caused by the bombs used to fight terrorism. Moreover, government agencies and their proxies all too often kill and frighten their own citizens, as happened when France's revolutionary government began devouring its own makers. Such killing can be a core policy of relatively stable governments as political philosopher Hannah Arendt pointed out in her analysis of Nazi Germany and Stalinist USSR in her book *Origins of Totalitarianism.*[11]

In recent years many governments are known to have supported death squads to eliminate and frighten opponents and some employ similar techniques against the people of other countries in order to weaken regimes they do not like or to assist regimes they favor that face internal opposition.

The US has been unusually open in admitting its use of secret operations. A law Congress passed in

1991 requiring the State Department to release documents about covert operations 30 years after the events has brought many interventions to light. For example, a document written by US Ambassador Marshall Green during the killings of hundreds of thousands of alleged communists in Indonesia in the wake of the US-approved coup that brought General Suharto to power in 1965 reveals that a list of communist leaders prepared by the US Embassy was given to the Indonesian Government in December 1965. Green writes, it 'is apparently being used by Indonesian security authorities who seem to lack even the simplest overt information on PKI [Indonesian Communist Party] leadership'. Another document shows that on 2 December 1965, Green endorsed a covert payment of 50 million rupiah to the Kap-Gestapu movement leading the repression.[12] US officials usually defend such operations as legitimate responses to requests for help from friendly governments or legitimate self-defense against foreign threats. They certainly do not call them terrorism.

Non-state terrorists are no strangers to posing and hypocrisy, although they typically have a smaller amplifier than do established governments. They, too, usually claim that their violence is not terror, but warfare. They also frequently lay claim to actions they did not commit and exaggerate their numbers and importance.

It is difficult to communicate in a straightforward way on a topic so morally polarized and so politically manipulated. Most people are highly suspicious of at least one side in the conflict. Moreover, the facts are ugly and the dangers are hair-raising. Yet the rewards of grappling with issues of terrorism are real and valuable. We gain a better understanding of the dangers we face from a frightening kind of violence and a deeper appreciation of the challenges facing politics, especially democratic politics. In these tough times we need to feel, we need to talk and we need to think. We can do all three at the same time. Such is the premise of this work.

A definition that works

Writers on terrorism frequently imply that laboring to define the term is pointless. They complain that hundreds of definitions have been proposed. They like to cite the dictum 'one person's terrorist is another person's freedom fighter', suggesting that to call someone a terrorist is to say no more than that one opposes their motivating cause. Much popular understanding, encouraged by common political use, takes the same position. People understand that the planners of the political violence carried out by non-governmental groups or by government agencies or their proxies claim their cause is just. Regimes that employ the ugly arts of murder and sabotage, often via proxy organizations, will never acknowledge that they are using terrorism. Those who speak for organizations that regularly use terror tactics avoid the term and claim they are resisting oppression and fighting for justice. Reuters press service and a few other news organizations rule out the use of the term on the grounds that it amounts to little more than moral labeling. Without a clear and pertinent definition the words 'terrorist' and 'terrorism' are counters in propaganda wars that obscure analysis of the frightful acts they are often used to describe.

Fortunately there is a simple and straightforward definition that corresponds to the idea of terrorism that most people hold. It has three elements: violence threatened or employed; against civilian targets; for political objectives. The writer Boaz Ganor, who has argued forcefully that an analytically useful definition is possible and imperative, proposes that 'terrorism is the intentional use of, or threat to use violence against civilians or against civilian targets, in order to attain political aims.' Unlike many other definitions this one

applies to governments (and their agencies and proxies) as well as to non-governmental groups and
individuals. It excludes nonviolent political actions
such as protests, strikes, demonstrations, tax revolts
and civil disobedience. It also excludes violent actions
against military and police forces. Many acts of guerrilla warfare or urban insurrection are not terrorism.[13]

Definitions that exclude state terrorism remain
blind to a major source of the violence and fear that is
visited on civilians around the world. State terrorism
and group terrorism, it is true, have rather different
features, but their effects on people and politics are
similar and they are often closely linked. They both fit
the basic idea of terrorism that most people hold: violence and threats of violence against civilians for
political ends.

According to our definition only actions are unam-
biguously terrorist or non-terrorist. People and
organizations and strategies make more or less use of
terrorism often in conjunction with other kinds of political action. How groups and states mix terrorism with
other kinds of action becomes an intriguing question.
Organizations that are designed to carry out terrorist
operations can properly be called terrorist organizations and the people who plan and implement the
actions are terrorists. The definition opens the door to
fundamental questions about the circumstances under
which people, groups and states adopt terrorist methods; the kind of people, groups and states that are
attracted to terrorist methods; and the consequences of
terrorist actions for victims and for perpetrators.

By focusing on a special kind of violence – violence
against civilians for political ends – the definition
acknowledges that many other kinds of violence sur-
round politics. Boaz Ganor believes that acceptance of
this definition and acceptance that terrorist acts are
morally wrong and politically destructive might
encourage organizations that use terrorism to choose
other means of struggle such as voting, demonstrating,

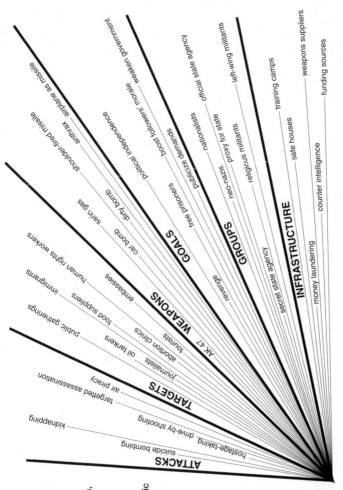

Array of terrorisms

There are many kinds of targets, weapons, groups, and supporting infrastructures. Every terrorist attack brings together a specific combination of these elements.

INFRASTRUCTURE
- training camps
- weapons suppliers
- safe houses
- funding sources
- counter intelligence
- money laundering
- secret state agency

GROUPS
- official state agency
- left-wing militants
- nationalists
- proxy for state
- neo-nazis
- religious militants
- secret state agency

GOALS
- weaken government
- boost followers morale
- political independence
- explicit demands
- free prisoners
- revenge

WEAPONS
- airplane as missile
- anthrax
- shoulder-fired missile
- dirty bomb
- sarin gas
- car bomb
- AK 47

TARGETS
- human rights workers
- immigrants
- public gatherings
- food suppliers
- oil tankers
- abortion clinics
- journalists
- tourists
- embassies

ATTACKS
- targeted assassination
- air piracy
- kidnapping
- hostage-taking
- drive-by shooting
- suicide bombing

Jonathan Barker

nonviolent resistance and guerrilla warfare. By his reasoning the violence of guerrilla warfare has the advantage over terrorism of being subject to the laws of war that, in principle, protect civilians and prisoners. Unfortunately, the record of guerrilla wars shows that both governments and guerrilla fighters often target civilians. Terrorism, much of it state terrorism, has been integral to guerrilla warfare, just as it has been part and parcel of state-on-state warfare. Removing terrorism from warfare is as big a challenge as is removing it from politics.

With this definition as a starting point we can begin a discussion of terrorism, but its terms will

---

Why it is hard to agree on the meaning of terrorism

At the Legal Committee's 29th Meeting in November 2000, several countries responded to the call to define terrorism.

Iran noted that some terrorists work under disguised names, including those of human rights NGOs to find safe haven in other nations. Iran also noted that technologies are creating new and surprising attacks against states unprepared to counter them. Finally, Iran noted that it was against an offer of immunity to military forces during times of peace as it was often these very forces which committed the atrocities.

Israel was particularly concerned that some states believed acts of bombing were not terrorism if done for national liberation. Without a standard of definition, without unified political will, terrorism thrives. The fight must be 'coordinated, continuous, comprehensive, and unrelenting.' GUUAM Group, former Soviet Republics, warned of connections between terrorism, aggressive separatism, and religious extremism. Like Israel, GUUAM warned that the objective of terrorism must be disconnected from the unjustifiable act.

Congo noted that state terrorism has allowed neighboring countries to pillage its people's natural resources. Yemen noted that terrorist attacks now seek to injure relationships between countries (like the US and Yemen after the bombing of the USS *Cole*). Syria joined in the call, and also noted that state terrorism by Israel had resulted in the deaths of Palestinian women and children. Further, Syria noted that Israel's chosen targets were often symbolic rather than military in nature, placing their actions under the umbrella of terrorism by some definitions. ■

United Nations Association of Michigan

require further elaboration. What counts as violence and as threat of violence? Who counts as civilian? What counts as a political objective? Lawmakers work these terms to design laws against terrorism that suit their purposes, often casting a very wide net indeed.

The definition allows one to raise the question of whether under some circumstances terrorism is justified much on the same lines that the doctrine of a just war is reasoned (see chapter four). If the objective is morally valid, the likelihood of success great and the cost in human suffering minimal, would not violence against civilians be morally justified?

More also needs to be said about the use of fear as a whip to bring about change in policies and organizations. What are the effects of the fear of terrorism? For what purposes is the manipulation of fear a useful tactic? The definition gets a vital discussion started.[14]

Questions

After September 11 a host of experts emerged who seemed to have thought about such questions. They were on the television night after night and the racks near the doors of bookstores began to fill with their publications.

For the most part, their focus and their starting point are different from those of this *Guide*. They tend to view terrorism exclusively in terms of the danger it poses to the US and to the West. They portray the terrorism of al-Qaeda or religious terrorism as implacably opposed to Western values and dedicated to damaging the governments and people who embody and defend those values. Often they want to place the current problem of terrorism in the context of how the US or the West has dealt with terrorism in the past. They set out to explain the new kinds of security measures that they now deem essential. Their rapid emergence shows how large and active the field of terrorism studies is. They have long worked behind the scenes. Even when terrorism dropped out of the headlines, these specialists lodged in universities, think-tanks, consulting firms, the press and government continued to write and to advise makers of policy.[15]

Terrorism specialists saw a failure of governments to adopt the intelligence and security measures they had long advocated. Every other conceivable interest and perspective also found a way to justify and illustrate its claims in terms of the events of September 11: Christian fundamentalists saw God's hand punishing America's moral corruption; opponents of US-led globalization saw payback for the economic and military domination of the global South; ecologists saw resource conflicts pushed to new heights; critics of social and economic policy saw a failure to meet the grievances of the poor and excluded; and heralds of cultural incompatibility saw Western values under attack. Some claims and perspectives seemed to gain in resonance, while others lost their voice. The idea of a 'clash of civilizations' was refurbished with grave enthusiasm while the idea of 'civil society' that had been making an impressive running for several years seemed to retreat to the sidelines. 'Imperialism' was resurrected from the graveyard of obsolete leftisms and reworked as a useful depiction of the responsibility of the US as the world's only superpower. It became apparent that one of the impacts of terrorism was its effect on the ideas through which political issues are defined, priorities are set and conflicts are conducted. How the current round of terrorism and counter-terrorism changes political discourse is a topic to explore.

One evident shift has been the move to greater secrecy and to restrictions of civil liberties on the part of the governments that lined up to fight the war on terrorism. Laws that constricted political liberties and legal rights were enacted with precious little debate and in very short order in Canada, the UK, Germany and elsewhere. It was a such powerful reflex that the bands of civil rights activists opposed to many of the new security measures had only limited success. How

Moveable mayhem

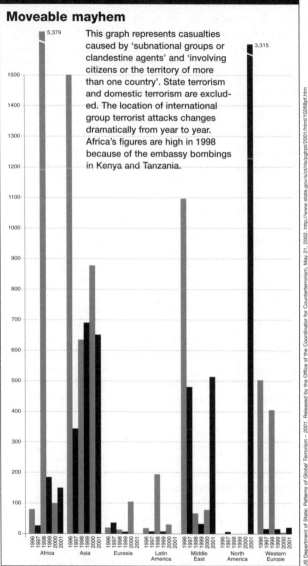

This graph represents casualties caused by 'subnational groups or clandestine agents' and 'involving citizens or the territory of more than one country'. State terrorism and domestic terrorism are excluded. The location of international group terrorist attacks changes dramatically from year to year. Africa's figures are high in 1998 because of the embassy bombings in Kenya and Tanzania.

US Department of State: *Patterns of Global Terrorism – 2001.* Released by the Office of the Coordinator for Counterterrorism, May 21, 2002. http://www.state.gov/s/ct/rls/pgtrpt/2001/html/10268pf.htm

corrosive to political liberties has counter-terrorism proved to be? Are authoritarian measures being exported to countries with weak democratic traditions to be used to block the groups beginning to establish activist democratic skills and practices? Do increased police powers and more intrusive intelligence methods make people more secure or even feel more secure?

These questions about political ideas and security measures are troubling. They sift down to one central issue: how do terrorism and the war on terrorism affect politics, popular politics in particular? Could the participant in the seminar on democracy mentioned above be right? Could the very actions, including the 'war on terrorism', that are intended to defend democracy in the US and other industrial countries undermine democracy in poorer and weaker countries? Could they also be working against democratic activism in the industrial North?

The reality of poverty, inequality and the crises of misdevelopment raise a second vital set of questions. People concerned about the extreme and growing inequality between and within countries frequently claim that it is one of the causes of terrorism. Many people in all classes in the countries of the South believe that a grave injustice is imposed on them by the economically and militarily powerful countries of Europe and North America led by the US. Television, film and travel make the huge inequalities in living conditions of the world's peoples more and more widely apparent. Moreover, the limited success of many peoples and cultures to better their material living conditions or to increase their capacity for autonomous evolution can be deeply humiliating, even for people who are not themselves poor or suffering. Is it not likely that the danger of terrorism will continue to fester and grow as long as the wounds of global inequality remain open and painful?

The connection of terrorism with violence, personal and society-wide security and painful injustice makes it particularly demanding to think about. These qualities generate emotional reactions. Paradoxically, the emotional coloring of the terrorism discussions offers a real opportunity to advance understanding once we get past the initial barriers to discussion and analysis. How can we really understand something we do not care about? Too many topics of real importance in our world today are met with so little passion that changes in understanding and therefore changes in conscious action are unlikely. Terrorism is different and it may carry us more deeply than we realize into questions about how our world works and fails to work.

The next chapter examines the kind of terrorism that is most discussed today – acts of violence against civilians for political objectives undertaken by groups and individuals unconnected with governments.

1 Kevin Toolis, 'Where suicide is a cult', *The Observer*, 16 December, 2001. **2** Adapted from Marcus Gee, 'The Dirty War's Dirtiest Soldier', *The Globe and Mail*, 10 June 2002 which cites 'Nunca Mas' the official report on the crimes of Argentina's Dirty War. **3** Daniel Howden, 'Found: the smoking gun that leads to a 'phantom' terror gang', *The Independent*, 3 July 2002. (http://news.independent.co.uk/europe/story.jsp?story=311430). **4** Amnesty International online. (http.www.amnesty.org/ailib/intcam/cemexico/salvador.htm). **5** Orphan Pamuk, 'The Anger of the Damned', *New York Review of Books*, 15 November 2001. **6** Jean Baudrillard, 'L'esprit du terrorisme', *Le Monde*, 3 November 2001. **7** Bush quotes from White House web site. (http://www.whitehouse.gov/news/releases/2001/09/). **8** Noam Chomsky, *9-11* (New York: Seven Stories Press, 2001). **9** Jeffrey C Goldfarb, 'Losing Our Best Allies in the War on Terrorism'. *New York Times*, 20 August 2002. **10** Lee Harris, 'Al-Qaeda's Fantasy Ideology', *Policy Review*, no. 114 (August and September 2002). **11** Hannah Arendt, *The Origins of Totalitarianism*, 2nd ed. (Cleveland: World Publishing Company, Meridian, 1958). **12** National Security Archive, Foreign Relations of the United States, 1964-68 Volume XXVI. (http://www.fas.org/sgp/advisory/state/NSAEBB52/NSAEBB52.html). **13** Boaz Ganor, 'Defining Terrorism: Is One Man's Terrorist Another Man's Freedom Fighter?' The International Policy Institute for Counter-Terrorism, 23 September 1998. (http://www.ict.org.il/). **14** Jorge Nef, 'Terrorismo: Política del Miedo'. *Relaciones Internacionales*, no. 7 (1984): 77-86. **15** For a critical view of the experts see: Edward S Herman and Gerry O'Sullivan, *The 'Terrorism' Industry the Experts and Institutions That Shape Our View of Terror* (New York: Pantheon Books, 1989).

2 Assessing the danger

Government leaders across the industrial world are ringing alarm bells about a new menace of terrorism. The cries of crisis, however, are not supported by facts about terrorist attacks gathered before September 11. But a few groups now have global ambitions and strategies and some of them seek the skill and the hardware to deploy biological, chemical or nuclear weapons.

SINCE THE EVENTS of 11 September 2001, US political leaders have been warning of the continuing high danger of terrorist outrages. On 3 December 2001, the day of the third officially-announced terrorist alert, a senior White House official told the Washington Post: 'There are al-Qaeda cells sitting out there – some in the United States, some in friendly countries, some in countries with a long history [of harboring terrorist groups]… This is the most dangerous fact for American security right now.' Three months later a US counter-terrorism official told *Time* magazine: 'It's going to be worse, and a lot of people are going to die. I don't think there's a damn thing we're going to be able to do about it.'

Officials anticipate a frightening range of attacks: food contamination, water supply poisoning, Hiroshima-size urban nuclear explosions, ocean tankers loaded with liquefied natural gas detonated in port cities, and bombings or suicide missions against buildings, bridges, airplanes, power plants, theme parks, monuments – wherever people gather. US government officials explain that the terrorists have no scruples; their goal is to kill as many people as possible. Terrorism experts note the vulnerability of many targets, the cheapness and wide availability of explosives, and the possible use of peaceful contrivances like passenger planes and nuclear generating plants as weapons. 'We're as vulnerable today as we were on 9/10 or 9/12,' said presidential counselor Karen Hughes. 'We just know more.' Given the range of possible attacks and their unpredictability, it is no wonder that 'vulnerable' describes how Americans feel.

Cheap and destructive

Like other crimes, terrorist attacks require a motive, a weapon and an opportunity. The warnings by officials and experts come from the recognition that weapons and opportunities are not difficult or costly to come by. The outlay for destroying a large building, an airplane or a ship is but a very small fraction of the expense of building or rebuilding it. And this calculation leaves out the emotional and material cost of lost lives and damaged families, communities, businesses and whole economies. The operation that bore such bitter fruit on 11 September 2001 cost maybe $500,000. The government aid package to compensate New York City for the damage it sustained comes to more than $20 billion with another $5 billion going to the families of victims. Estimates of the damage to buildings and their contents alone go much higher, and there is the Pentagon damage to add in as well. If the cost of the action was

Osama bin Laden estimates 'destructive return' of twin towers attack

In a video tape first aired on 17 April, 2002 Osama bin Laden reveals that he, too, is interested in calculating the dollar value of the destruction wrought on September 11 and in the ripple effects on the global economy. 'More than $1 trillion in losses resulted from these successful and blessed attacks and may God bless these martyrs and welcome them to paradise.' He also gives figures for job losses, the drop in share values on Wall Street, and loss of productivity. For those who think like bin Laden the weakened value of stocks traded in New York (at least through December 2002) and the scandals about accounting practices and payments to corporate executives confirm both the impact of the terrorist threat and the immorality at the heart of American economic power. ■

Reuters

In many countries there is little or no terrorism

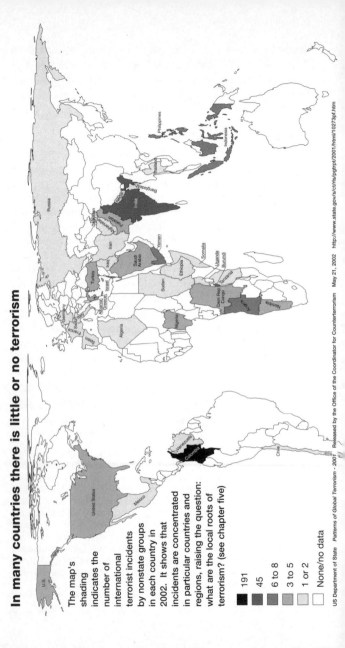

The map's shading indicates the number of international terrorist incidents by nonstate groups in each country in 2002. It shows that incidents are concentrated in particular countries and regions, raising the question: what are the local roots of terrorism? (see chapter five)

- ■ 191
- 45
- 6 to 8
- 3 to 5
- 1 or 2
- □ None/no data

US Department of State Patterns of Global Terrorism - 2001 Released by the Office of the Coordinator for Counterterrorism May 21, 2002 http://www.state.gov/s/ct/rls/pgtrpt/2001/html/10273pf.htm

$500,000 and the damage is estimated at $50 billion then the 'rate of destructive return' was 100,000 to 1.

Admittedly this was a spectacular event and the figures are only indicative. However, they make the point: a terrorist attack can do a lot of damage at a low cost. Figures are harder to come by for terrorist attacks elsewhere, but there can be no doubt that the principle is universal. The war on terrorism in all its dimensions may have made it more difficult and costly for terrorists to enter critical locations and to cross national boundaries, but it is hard to see how the low cost of weapons and the availability of opportunity can be altered fundamentally. What then about motive?

Bin Laden demonstrates a deep interest in building support for his goals. His videos and audio tapes seek to create and to strengthen motives for more terrorist attacks. They express disgust at the continued presence of Western forces in the holy lands of Islam and anger at the plight of the Palestinian people. Opinion polling in Muslim countries suggests that al-Qaeda is cultivating fertile ground; a large current of opinion is critical of the US. Gallup interviewed almost 10,000 people during December 2001 and January 2002 in its first-ever large-scale opinion polling in nine predominantly Muslim countries – Indonesia, Iran, Jordan, Kuwait, Lebanon, Morocco, Pakistan, Saudi Arabia and Turkey. The dominant image of the US was a country that is 'ruthless, aggressive, conceited, arrogant, easily provoked and biased.' Opinion of the US was 53 per cent unfavorable and 22 per cent favorable and the view of President Bush was even less favorable.[1] Hostile opinion is one ingredient in the mix of motives, attitudes and interests out of which terrorism grows.

Local and regional grievances are more common than the global ones that al-Qaeda seeks to reinforce. They are often enduring and emotionally charged as well. Many have given rise to armed action that includes terrorism. Certain anti-colonial nationalist movements after the Second World War used violence

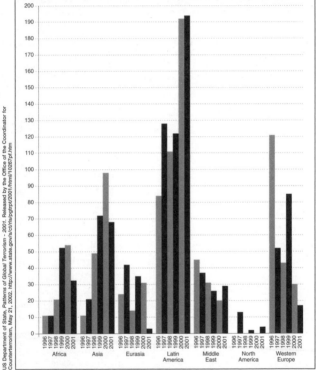

In sheer number of terrorist attacks, Latin America stands out

From 1996 to 2001 the number of attacks was rising in Africa, Asia and Latin America, while it was falling in Europe, Eurasia, the Middle East and North America. Domestic and state terrorism are not included.

against civilians: for example, the FLN in Algeria and Mau Mau or the Land and Freedom Army in Kenya. Tamils in Sri Lanka, Palestinians in the Middle East, Basques in Spain, Corsicans in France, Catholics in Northern Ireland, Kurds in Iraq and Turkey and Sikhs in India are groups associated with episodes of terrorism in nationalist movements seeking independence from existing nation-states. Militant Islamic groups that have adopted terrorist tactics have been active in Algeria, Egypt, Lebanon, Palestine, Pakistan, Kashmir, Afghanistan, Saudi Arabia, Dubai and several other countries.

Groups with many other kinds of entrenched political and moral agendas have given rise to episodes of terrorist action. They include, for example, white supremacists and right-wing militias in the US; left-wing militants in Italy, Germany and Colombia; rural movements in Peru and Uganda. Add to them Haganah, Irgun and the Stern Gang with their differing agendas for the creation of Israel and EOKA (*Ethniki Organosis Kyprion Agoniston*) supporting union of Cyprus with Greece and the full spectrum of terrorist organizations starts to take shape.

Motivation for terrorism is plentiful, diverse and widespread. Almost every country has some potential for generating groups with terrorist tendencies.

Why are terrorist attacks so rare?

Anyone who thinks about the possibility of a terrorist attack senses how vulnerable we are in public places, work sites, and even at home. Full protection is simply impossible. If a driving motive is also present, fear of terrorist attacks seems only rational. Motive, weapon and opportunity are all too prevalent. For groups willing to use terrorism, the temptation must be great to at least issue the threat.

Yet group terrorism is relatively rare and its most deadly and disruptive episodes are localized. Statistically it is well down on the list of the dangers people face, somewhere between bee stings and lightning strikes as a cause of death. Why are such attacks so rare? Are they likely to increase?

Part of the answer lies in the fact that much of the time terrorist acts fail to advance the objectives their perpetrators seek. Those who engage in terrorism usually intend more than material damage and the spreading of death and mayhem. They seek to over-throw governments or at least to change their policies. While spreading mayhem is relatively easy, under most conditions the chances of achieving political objectives by doing so are small. Governments rarely change pol-icy in response to terrorism, at least not in the direction terrorists desire. Instead they resist, often ferociously. People who commit themselves to terrorism have to believe either that their case is exceptional, or that the action is so crucial the odds do not matter. Some may believe that provoking a savage response will awaken people for the next round of struggle.

Even if this logic is right, the success gained is cost-ly and guarantees no early victory, only continuing conflict. So the odds against any real political success are a clear deterrent for adherents of political move-ments who might be tempted into terrorism. The Palestinian intellectual and public figures who pub-lished an 'urgent appeal to stop the suicide bombings' on 20 June 2002 pointed to the problem. They argued that the bombings 'deepen the hatred... between the Palestinian and Israeli people. Also they destroy the possibility of peaceful coexistence between them in two neighboring states [and] do not contribute towards achieving our national project that calls for freedom and independence.'

Terrorist tactics stand the best chance where a gov-ernment has lost legitimacy in the eyes of the people it governs. The most striking of these successes are the nationalist movements against colonialism or cultural-nationalist movements of large populations resisting domination by other peoples or cultures. Once colo-nial powers recognized they could no longer hold their empires, violence or threats of violence often accelerated their departure.

Terrorists with special agendas such as opposition to abortion or to racial mixing may count their actions successful if they gain publicity for their cause and recruit a few new adherents. Some of them seem to take satisfaction in performing what they consider to be a difficult, but highly moral, act.

Moral and legal barriers

According to all ordinary moral codes terrorist acts are wrong. Strong social controls and moral strictures work against terror tactics. Destroying private or public property is already stepping beyond the limit of most morality and the law; threatening and killing people is a big step beyond that. Activists, even those who turn to violence to pursue political objectives, are often reluctant to target civilians. All major religions teach that killing is rarely justified. The moral code of almost all families and friendship groups frowns on murder. All the social pressures and powers of law enforcement that discourage other kinds of crime also work against terrorism. The physical pressures are very real too: suspected terrorists can be arrested, tried and

Terrorism compared to other risks of death 1996-1999

	1996	1997	1998	1999
Terrorism[1]				
Africa	80	28	5,379	185
Asia	1,507	344	635	690
Eurasia	20	27	12	8
Latin America	18	11	195	9
Middle East	1,097	480	68	31
Western Europe	503	17	405	16
US	0	7	0	0
World total	3,225	914	6,694	939
Other causes (US only)[2]				
Rabies Infections	6,982	8,105	7,259	na
Road Traffic Deaths	42,065	42,013	41,501	41,611
Pedestrian Deaths	5,449	5,321	5,228	4,906
Murder	19,650	18,210	16,970	15,530

[1] US Department of State, *Patterns of Global Terrorism 2001*, May 21, 2002.
[2] Roger D Congleton, 'Terrorism, Interest-Group Politics, and Public Policy: Curtailing Criminal Modes of Political Speech', *The Independent Review 7*, 1 (Summer 2002): 59.

punished. They are likely to suffer long detentions, tough questioning (often torture) and severe punishment, including death.

The moral code against attacking, injuring and killing civilians also works against the use of terrorism as 'propaganda of the deed'. The public is more likely to be repelled by the shedding of blood than it is to be impressed by the urgency of the terrorists' cause.

Alternatives often exist

Given the statistical, moral, legal and physical disincentives, it is not surprising that most political activists choose other avenues of action and protest – contesting elections and organizing strikes, mounting mass demonstrations or going on hunger campaigns. Where governments have closed off other channels, activists may find the path of violence the best alternative. Even then many will prefer to attack police posts, government offices and army camps rather than to target civilians. For many guerrilla warfare is a better choice than terrorism.

The adoption of terrorist strategies can precipitate acrimonious splits in protest organizations. Opponents of terrorism will point out that choosing such tactics only takes energy away from other kinds of politics and undermines legitimate action. It also opens the way to criticism by condoning violence against innocent people. Some of the most effective critics of terrorism are activists whose goals are the same as those of the advocates of terrorism, but who endorse only nonviolent means to achieve them.

A group undertaking terrorist action needs material support as well as moral justification. Although the budget for a basic terrorist operation is not large, it takes effort, money and skill to assemble arms, bomb-making supplies, training and ways of organizing. It is difficult to estimate the budget of al-Qaeda, but it was certainly no greater than the military spending of a small state. At points it had several training camps in

Sudan, Afghanistan, Philippines and Indonesia with buildings, computers, satellite telephones, weapons, munitions, rudimentary laboratories and medical facilities. It could count on a large financial flow from wealthy Saudi donors and far-flung charity organizations. It could buy airplane tickets, pay training fees and cover the living expenses of members of many associated cells operating in expensive cities in Spain, Germany, France, Belgium, Netherlands, Italy, Britain, and the US and also in less expensive countries like Pakistan.

At the other end of the spectrum, it took the five Canadian activists who called themselves 'Direct Action' more than a year in the early 1980s to steal the necessary weapons, explosives and cash; do research on targets; design and build timing devices; and train in handling arms. Only then were they able to plant their first bomb at Dunsmuir electrical power station on Vancouver Island.[2]

During the Cold War, terrorist groups might gain support from governments on one side or the other, sometimes even from both. Groups probably still get most of their funding from governments. Big powers may fund them to quietly weaken or replace troublesome rulers of a smaller power. Small powers may be interested in undermining a hostile neighboring regime. Terrorists can also tap other sources: business interests; the clandestine trade of drugs or diamonds; crimes such as kidnapping, theft and credit-card fraud; and remittances from supporters, often members of diaspora communities who identify with a cause. Because terrorism always has this economic side, those who control the flow of funding have considerable control over the strength of terrorist activity. And there is always the possibility that terrorism will become a business with the flow of income an end in itself.

Hard to justify

Despite all the barriers, groups do undertake terrorism, sometimes on a large scale, as the case of the

Assessing the danger

Liberation Tigers of Tamil Eelam (LTTE) shows. In their fight to carve an independent Tamil state out of the northern part of Sri Lanka they have created an effective guerrilla army and resisted attacks by the Sri Lankan and Indian armies. The LTTE has also directed hundreds of terrorist actions against government and military leaders, moderate Tamil politicians, rival Tamil guerrilla leaders, leaders of the Muslim minority and economic facilities staffed with workers and surrounded by crowds. Their 150 to 200 suicide bombings since 1983 can claim some spectacular results, including the murder of Prime Minister Rajiv Gandhi of India (1991) and President Ranasinghe Premadasa of Sri Lanka (1993). In 1996 in front of the Central Bank of Sri Lanka they detonated a suicide truck bomb powerful enough to kill 88 and injure 1,400.

Successful terrorism

• As for the futility of terrorism itself, who could say with confidence that Jewish terrorism – the assassination of Lord Moyne and then of Count Bernadotte, the bombing of the King David Hotel, followed by selective massacres in a few Palestinian villages in order to secure the flight of all Palestinians – did not succeed in dislodging the British and consolidating Jewish control of the new state? Though terror alone did not create the state of Israel – the moral legitimacy of the claim of the Holocaust survivors counted even more – terror was instrumental, and terror worked. ■
Michael Ignatieff, 'The Lessons of Terror: All War Against Civilians Is Equal', *The New York Times Book Review*, 17 February 2002

• President Bush and his spokespeople have repeatedly assured us that, if we are resolute, terrorism cannot succeed. But the actual record of guerrilla warfare or terrorism since the Second World War is that it has always brought colonial, occupying powers to the negotiating table. That was so for the British Empire in Kenya, Cyprus, Aden and twice in Ireland; for the French in Vietnam, Algeria and recently even in Corsica; for the Spanish vis-à-vis the Basques; for the Dutch in the East Indies; and for the Americans themselves in Vietnam. Indeed the Americans used the tactic in the 18th century against the British. And it seems likely that in the end the Israelis will reap the same reward in Palestine. ■
John Downey, 'The West against terrorism', www.opendemocracy.co.uk, 25 April 2002

A statement of the president of the LTTE illustrates the problem faced by anyone attempting publicly to justify terrorism. Velupillai Prabhakaran claimed in a speech on 27 November 2001 that groups like his were not 'terrorist' because they used violence 'for a concrete political objective'. The global battle against terrorism, he asserted, should target 'real terrorists'. 'Western democratic nations should provide a clear and comprehensive definition of the concept of terrorism that would distinguish between freedom struggles based on the right to self-determination and blind terrorist acts based on fanaticism.'[3]

A more honest and consistent approach was taken by Prime Minister Mahathir Mohamad of Malaysia at the meeting of the foreign ministers of the Organization of the Islamic Conference (OIC) in March 2002. 'Whether the attackers are acting on their own or on the orders of their governments, whether they are regulars or irregulars, if the attack is against civilians, then they must be considered as terrorists.' The OIC disagreed with Mahathir and failed to arrive at an agreed definition of terrorism. The problem they faced is evident in their decision to 'reject any attempt to link terrorism to the struggle of the Palestinian people in the exercise of their inalienable right to establish their independent state…'[4]

Defenders of terrorism (who may not use the term) make several other arguments besides that of 'just struggle'. They note the absence of other means of action; claim that the people attacked are not really civilians (they are soldiers since they support a government or an army engaged in repression). They suggest that the people are themselves criminals or murderers or even not fully human – savage, uncivilized, monstrous, irreligious or evil and not entitled to full human rights. Some groups deny that they target civilians, or even people, at all.

The difficulty of justifying terrorist acts on either moral or practical grounds presents a problem for recruiters of future terrorists. Several kinds of justification need to work together in a receptive environment before many people will join up. Chapter five will explore some of the features of a receptive environment. But the appeal is undoubtedly greater for people who feel humiliated, disempowered and disadvantaged and who see no alternative to a violent course of action.

Some terrorism is always likely to occur at the edge of politics. Political order and loyalty extend only so far. A political grievance, an experience of oppression or neglect, a failure of security, or a religious revival will push some people over the edge to a place where the rules of civic security no longer apply. To know that terrorism is always possible leaves unanswered the question of why it flares up and persists in certain times and places. It also fails to explain whether terrorism is now a growing danger that should preoccupy governments and citizens alike. A brief account of some examples of religious, nationalist and political terrorist episodes will help to clarify how to approach these questions.

Religious militants

Some of the earliest episodes of terrorism are connected with religious movements. Well before the establishment of modern, secular nation-states the ambition to give political expression to religious commitments was a source of conflict and a problem that plagued pluralistic states and empires. Three words common in the vocabulary of reporting on terrorism derive from religious activism: zealot, assassin and thug. Stories associated with these words illustrate forms and motives of violence that still are found at the edge of politics.

Zealots. The zealots were radical defenders of a purist version of Jewish religion and political autonomy after Rome established its rule over Judaea. They stood firmly against the legalistic and scholarly Pharisees and the élitist Sadducees, who compromised with Roman rule. They used guerrilla and terrorist tactics against the Romans and members of competing political and religious groups among the Jews.

Assassins. 'Hashish takers' (hasashin) was the name given by their political detractors to the Nizari Ismailis. A kinder etymology says they called themselves 'assassiyun' designating people faithful to the 'assass' or foundations of Islam.[5] Late in the 11th century the group broke off from the Shi'a branch of Islam that had established a caliphate in Cairo to rival the Sunni Abissid caliphate in Baghdad. For almost two centuries it disputed the legitimacy of both caliphates and kept alive an Ismaili resistance to the domination of the Seljuk Turk overlords. Under its founding leader, Hassan Sabbah, the group seized the large mountain fort at Alumat in Persia. They collected tolls from caravans in return for protection. Their purist doctrine of Islam emphasized submission to the leader's authority and the justice of murdering prominent enemies. Trained killers armed with daggers were sent to commit the murders, fully expecting to be caught and executed for their pious action.

Thugs. As the colonial government in India consolidated its hold on the subcontinent in the early 1830s, it faced a persistent problem of robbery and murder. British investigators attributed a large part of the crime to a special category of criminals known as 'thugs' or 'thuggees', members of an enduring secret society of devotees of the Hindu deity of destruction, Kali. The British believed that the religious commitment of this hereditary sect required that they strangle travellers in a ritually prescribed manner. The ritual side of their violence seems to have displaced any political goal it may have once had. A recent review of the evidence concludes that thuggee was by far the longest-lasting and most murderous of all terrorist organizations, killing some half-million people over a period of at least 400 years.[6]

Assessing the danger

Several of the most active and persistent bouts of terrorism in recent times are connected with religion. Like zealots and assassins some militant Christians, Sikhs, Muslims, Hindus, Jews and adherents of other religions have the conviction that their religious calling

Justifying terrorism

Timothy McVeigh on the Oklahoma City bombing: 'What the US Government did at Waco and Ruby Ridge was dirty, and I gave dirty back to them at Oklahoma City.' ■
ABC News

Palestinian jailed in Israel for terrorist acts: 'Armed actions have a goal. Even if civilians are killed, it's not because we like it or are bloodthirsty, it is a fact of life in a people's struggle. The group doesn't do it because it wants to kill civilians but because the jihad must go on.' ■
From interviews in Israeli jails made by Jerrold M Post, Australian Broadcasting Company, 22 October 2001

World Islamic Front Statement: Jihad Against Jews and Crusaders. 'The ruling to kill the Americans and their allies – civilians and military – is an individual duty for every Muslim who can do it in any country in which it is possible to do it, in order to liberate the al-Aqsa Mosque and the holy mosque [Mecca] from their grip, and in order for their armies to move out of all the lands of Islam, defeated and unable to threaten any Muslim. This is in accordance with the words of Almighty Allah, "and fight the pagans all together as they fight you all together," and "fight them until there is no more tumult or oppression, and there prevail justice and faith in Allah."' ■
Sheikh Osama bin-Muhammad bin-Laden; Ayman al-Zawahiri, emir of the Jihad Group in Egypt; Abu-Yasir Rifa'i Ahmad Taha, Egyptian Islamic Group; Sheikh Mir Hamzah, secretary of the Jamiat-ul-Ulema-e-Pakistan; Fazlur Rahman, emir of the Jihad Movement in Bangladesh, 23 February 1998

Paul J Hill, convicted murderer of Dr John Britton and volunteer abortion clinic escort James Barrett in 1994: 'I well remember (prior to the shooting) the oppressive feeling of realizing that I was not free to defend my neighbors as Christ requires... The fear of being persecuted for disobeying our tyrannical government made submitting to its yoke seem attractive... It required an act of the will to even consider obeying the Lord. The inner joy and peace that have flooded my soul since I have cast off the State's tyranny makes my little cell a triumphant and newly liberated kingdom. ■
Letter to the White Rose Banquet in honor of the sacrifices made by anti-abortion activists in prison, 22 December 1997

requires violent defense against its enemies. Where most people see terrorism against innocent civilians some religious militants will see a just war against agents of evil. The parallels with pre-modern terrorism are striking. But there is one important difference. The original zealots, assassins, and thugs arose in times and places where the ideal of secular politics was not an alternative to political religions. The conflict was about which religious interpretation would govern politics.

The large majority of the adherents of the major religions that have produced terrorist offshoots do not support terrorism. The militants who believe their religion demands terrorist actions always face two sets of enemies: those outside the religion and their co-religionists who oppose the use of terror. Both have become targets of terrorist attacks.

Two kinds of terrorists in the US cite Christian doctrine as justification for their action. One is driven by its abhorrence of abortion. Reverend Michael Bray served four years in prison for destroying seven abortion clinics in the region around Washington DC in the 1980s. His book, *A Time to Kill*, advocates the use against abortionists of 'defensive force', a euphemism for assassination.[7] His particular doctrine, Dominion Theology, holds that Christianity must establish the dominion of God over politics and society. Other activists in the radical antiabortion movement follow Reconstruction Theology with its aim of forming a fully theocratic Christian state. It traces its intellectual heritage to the ideas of John Calvin.

The other US Christian movement that supports terrorism, Christian Identity (see p 94), foresees a revolution led by European whites that will overthrow the evil and duplicitous Zionist Occupation Government (they call it 'ZOG') and establish a racially-pure society governed by biblical laws. Some members form communities, like Elohim City in Oklahoma, where they practice and teach their doctrines and train for the coming conflict. Timothy

McVeigh, who was executed for killing 168 people in the Oklahoma City bombing of 1995, had a connection with Elohim City.[8]

Africa, with its strong traditions of belief in ancestral and other spirits, has been fertile territory for prophetic Christian movements. Under weak and conflict-ridden governments a few of them have turned to violence. In northern Uganda in 1986, for example, a prophetic Christian movement led by Alice Lakwena joined with rebel soldiers to form the Holy Spirit Mobile Force (HSMF). For a time it was a serious local threat to the Uganda Defence Force, with soldiers recruited in the south, but it was weakened when Alice Lakwena was forced to flee to Kenya.

Terrorism expanded when Joseph Kony claimed Lakwena's prophetic mantle and revived fighting with a group called the Lord's Resistance Army (LRA). It has destroyed dozens of villages, schools and granaries and abducted thousands of children, forcing the boys to become fighters and the girls sex slaves. Over time its claim to represent a religious movement has evaporated. It is now widely considered a horror perpetuated for the benefit of a few leaders and the convenience of the Sudanese Government which uses it to fight the rebels in southern Sudan and to trouble the government of Uganda.[9]

Movements that advocate the use of violence to enforce their reading of Christian doctrine or to promote the advent of their kind of theocratic government are likely to persist as relatively minor movements vying for power in specific states.

Islam, like Christianity, boasts a large number of differing doctrines competing for attention and adherents. The leading ideas for renewing the political expression of Islam came after the Second World War from activists in Egypt and Pakistan who opposed the trend to secular nationalism. In Egypt in the 1950s and 1960s President Abdel Gamal Nasser came down hard on Muslim writers and activists like Hasan al-Banna who founded the Muslim Brotherhood, and Sayyid Qutb, an influential writer and leading advocate of a purified Islam. They joined Mawlana Mawdudi, founder in Pakistan of Jamaat-i-Islami (Islamic Assembly), in wanting the Muslim world to achieve scientific and technical progress on its own terms within a state created to reflect the teachings of Islam.

For these activists the founding of Israel, the millions of Palestinian refugees and the unemployment and poverty of Muslim societies were stark evidence of the failure of secular nationalism in the Middle East and the Muslim world. Mawdudi was troubled by the colonialist (British and French) threat to Muslim identity and to pan-Islamic unity. For him the secular nationalism promoted by leaders like Gandhi and Nehru in India and Sukarno in Indonesia was just another face of Western influence.

Along with Ayatollah Khomeini in Iran, Qutb and Mawdudi developed an activist ideology with a specific form of Islam as the all-inclusive guide for individuals and countries facing change and disruption. They teach that the Qur'an, the example of Muhammad's own life and the early Muslim community are the models to follow. Islamic law is the template for Muslim political structures. Social revolution and scientific progress must be pursued within Islam and not by borrowing Western ideas and values. To construct a true Islamic society means engaging in a personal and a political struggle or jihad for true Islam in an environment polluted by ignorance, greed and immorality, a condition Qutb termed 'jahiliyya'. Muslim governments that fail to implement sharia law and true Islam are as much a part of jahiliyya as the Western societies that have defiled Islam from the time of the crusades.[10]

The modern calls for a pure and political Muslim community bear some resemblance to the call issued by the Wahhabi movement of purified Islam that was founded 250 years ago by Muhammad ibn Abd al-Wahhab and is the official religion of Saudi Arabia. Although Islamic activists criticize the Saudi rulers for flouting in practice their puritanical official doctrines, they benefit from the hundreds of institutes, schools and *madrassas* (seminaries) founded by the Saudi Government to promote Wahhabism from Africa to Indonesia.

In the late 1960s and the 1970s several leaders and associations dedicated to Islamic reform in Egypt, Lebanon and Palestine reinforced the tendency to use violence against their governments, accusing them of betraying Islam. Their critique of the ruling groups became more bitter and their actions more violent after the debâcle of the 1967 Arab-Israeli war and loss of land and dignity.

The internationalist version of the movement for purified Islam received a great boost after 1979, the year of the Iranian revolution and the hostage-taking at the US embassy in Teheran. The US, in an effort to turn some of the energy of the Islamic revival against Soviet power in Central Asia, became one of the main boost-ers. Pervez Amir Ali Hoodbhoy explains: 'With Pakistan's Mohammed Zia ul-Haq as America's fore-most ally, the CIA openly recruited Islamic holy warriors from Egypt, Saudi Arabia, Sudan and Algeria. Radical Islam went into overdrive as its superpower ally and mentor funneled support to the mujaheddin; Ronald Reagan feted them on the White House lawn.'[11] The Saudis and Pakistan's Inter Service Intelligence Agency (ISI) collaborated in the project. The US saw a double payoff. Thwarting the Soviets in Afghanistan was as attractive as diverting militant Islam away from the Middle East to fight in Afghanistan.[12] The withdrawal of the Soviets from Afghanistan in February 1989 was a dramatic turning point. What appeared to be an unal-loyed victory for the US-Saudi strategy of diverting and controlling the new energies of militant Islam was in reality the beginning of a newly transnational terrorist force.

There was, as well, an explosion of new Islamic organizations and movements in other countries that fed on the impatience of urban youth, many of them poor, for the jobs and material benefits that their governments were failing to deliver. Two examples: During the *Intifada* that began 1987 in Palestine, Hamas, with its social service branches and its hardline opposition to Israel, became a powerful rival to Yasser Arafat's secular PLO. In the early 1990s in Algeria the Islamic Salvation Front mounted a strong political and electoral challenge to the nationalist government in Algiers. Only a military coup and a wrenching civil war kept it from power. Governments, wanting to foster rivals to the movements they most feared, often supported the radical Muslim organizations in their early days. President Sadat of Egypt supported militant Muslim associations as a counterweight to left-wing movements, but it was a member of one such association who assassinated him in 1981. Israel gave quiet support to the precursor of Hamas in Gaza in order to weaken Yassar Arafat's Fatah organization only to see Hamas become one of its most implacable Palestinian opponents during the first *Intifada* that erupted in 1987.[13]

The experience of the tens of thousands of Muslim youth from a dozen countries who studied and trained to fight in Afghanistan reinforced an internationalist current in the new activism. Although the ideas that guided the formation of the camps derived from the tradition of Qutb and Mawdudi as well as Wahhabism, the training seems to have been much more limited and quite instrumental. It was aimed at creating a loyal, unquestioning and effective force committed to fight against both the corrupted governments of the Islamic world and the centers of global dominance in the US and Europe. The multinational experience of training, fighting and winning made it possible for certain ambitious militant leaders to imagine new kinds of attacks on the 'forces of evil' and to find people willing and able to carry them out.

Nationalists without a state

Nationalism, like religion, can rouse intense political passions. The redrawing of political boundaries as empires were reformed into nation-states, first in Europe and then in Europe's colonial empires inaugurated a long period of bloody political turmoil. The question of which group's cultural identity will gain political expression is still hotly contested in many places. Most existing states are home to a plurality of cultures and language groups. Some members of some of these groups hear the voice of national destiny and agitate for their own new separate state.

Bent on achieving nationhood, movements usually organize much like states, with governing committees, administrative hierarchies and armies. Conflict with the existing state is inevitable and the pull toward violent conflict is strong. It tends to take the form of guerrilla warfare, but terrorism is an ever-present possibility. In some places it becomes an important, even defining, element in the struggle.

Western Europe and North America, despite their relatively old and well-established nation-states, harbor several unresolved nationalist claims. The movements that have made the greatest use of violence against civilians are the Irish Republican movement (the IRA and its offshoots) and Basque Homeland and Liberty (*Euzkadi Ta Azkatasuna* or ETA). Other movements like the *Front de Libération de Quebec* (FLQ) and the National Liberation Front of Corsica (FLNC) have resorted to terrorism from time to time.

The case of ETA illustrates how nationalist terrorism comes about. ETA grew out of the Basque Nationalist Party that since 1894 had stood for preserving and increasing the legal autonomy that the Basque regions of Spain and France had retained since the Middle Ages. The nationalists suffered heavy repression under

Franco's authoritarian and centralizing rule in post-war Spain. Basque autonomy was abolished and the nationalist leadership went into exile in Paris. When political demonstrations and other nonviolent action produced no gains, a group of younger nationalists in 1959 founded ETA with the intention of using the tactics of anti-colonial nationalist movements to win Basque independence. As long as ETA was fighting Spain's fascist government the use of violence had much support in the Basque region and from democrats in other regions of Spain and in other countries. That did not prevent the organization from splitting into nationalist and revolutionary socialist wings with the revolutionaries willing to use sabotage and assassination as tactics of struggle. Their main targets were government officials, politicians and military forces.

In a dramatic action in 1973 ETA assassinated Franco's presumed successor, Admiral Luis Carrero Blanco. Their action probably hastened the end of the fascist dictatorship. It also initiated what ETA calls the 'action-reprisal-action' cycle. The regime sent in the troops to punish the perpetrators and set off a lengthy regional war. A decade of active terrorism ensued. In 1980, their bloodiest year, ETA killed 118 people. Once democratic rights were established in Spain and once the Basque region was accorded some autonomy, ETA's policy lost public support and became disputed within the movement. Yet a core of die-hard fighters for independence refused offers of amnesty and eluded arrest.

Ceasefire

Influenced by the experience of the Irish Republican Army, ETA declared a ceasefire in September 1998 and called upon the political wing of Basque nationalism to negotiate self-determination. By then they had killed almost 800 people, more than half of them Spanish soldiers and police. The Spanish Government continued making arrests and ETA proceeded with attacks against property and raids on arms depots.

After little more than a year ETA declared the peace process 'blocked and poisoned' and announced that after 3 December 1999 it would 'reactivate the armed struggle.' Although the organization is estimated to comprise only about 20 active members and 100 supporters, it claims to have killed 38 people since ending the ceasefire. Each attack now provokes a counter demonstration.[14] On 2 March 2002 organizers said that 50,000 demonstrators marched in the Basque coastal town of Portugalete to protest an attack attributed to ETA: a bomb placed in a shopping cart that injured socialist politician Esther Cabezudo and her bodyguard Enrique Torres.

At the heart of the idea of the nation-state lies an irreducible ambiguity: the 190 states that have come into existence are far from reflecting all the cultural groups that do or that might express a national political calling. Oppressed and unrecognized cultures continue to voice political aspirations, and sometimes splinter off groups that engage in terrorism in the name of their claim: Kurds in Turkey, Iran and Iraq, Sikhs in India, Acehnese in Indonesia, Albanians in Kosovo, and many others.

Movements of the Left and Right

Groups moved by political ideology are not trying to redraw state boundaries; their goal is to change the institutions and policies of government and to put new kinds of people in power. Disputes between dissidents and governments on such matters is the stuff of normal political conflict, but oppositional groups sometimes choose to employ terror in addition to or instead of other forms of action. During the Cold War groups in several Western capitalist countries adopted sabotage, assassination and bombings as forms of action.

Italy in the 1970s, for example, experienced an especially active period of violence. Its impact was greatest on 16 March 1978 when members of Italy's Red Brigades kidnapped Aldo Moro, leader of the

Christian Democratic Party and five-time premier of Italy. They chose the day of the 'historic compromise' between the Christian Democrats and the Italian Communist Party (PCI), an arrangement avidly opposed by the Red Brigades who saw themselves as true followers of revolutionary Marxism-Leninism long abandoned by the PCI. Founded in Milan in 1970 by Renato Curcio and Margherita Cagol, the Red Brigades grew out of a Marxist study group at the University of Trento. Their violence started with fire-bombing industrial targets and then expanded to kidnapping, knee-capping and, finally, murder. The kidnapping and eventual murder of Aldo Moro was the apex of left-wing political violence in Italy, but terrorist acts continued into the 1980s. Between 1970 and 1982 the Red Brigades claimed responsibility for over 2000 illegal acts in which 161 people were killed.

The Red Brigades were only the most enduring of many similar organizations: 537 differently named groups with some continuity of existence have been counted in Italy during those years. Another 199 people were killed in terrorist acts not claimed by the Red Brigades. In the mid-1980s the Red Brigades were fading. Arrests, internal divisions, defections via amnesty and ideological crisis weakened them. In 1984 four leaders in prison published a letter abandoning armed struggle: 'The international conditions that made this struggle possible no longer exist.'[15]

The file is not closed on the Red Brigades: in March 2002 after the well-orchestrated murder of an economic adviser to Italy's right-wing government, a long document signed by the Red Brigades for the Construction of a Combatant Communist Party was published on the internet taking credit for the 'execution'. A similar crime with a similar claim was committed in 1999. Italians feared that another generation of Red Brigades violence was in the offing.

The Red Brigades are an example of left-wing terrorism that fit the ideological contestation of the Cold

War. Other examples include the Red Army Faction (often called Baader-Meinhof Gang) in Germany, the Weather Underground in the US and Direct Action in Canada. The latter two tried to confine their violence to property and many of their members would deny that they were terrorists. Although these organizations identified with the Marxist Left, they broke from the old-Left idea that action must be based on an analysis of class forces and on organized support from the working class. What the old Left saw as rejecting naive 'voluntarism' looked to the new revolutionaries as a failure of nerve when social conditions demanded action.

More common in the United States has been the right-wing terrorism of white supremacist groups like the Ku Klux Klan and Aryan Nation and populist armed militias convinced that Jewish-communist-capitalists have turned the federal government and the UN into engines of oppression. In the US Louis Beam, a prominent white supremacist, promoted a tactic of 'leaderless resistance' in which 'phantom cells' of small groups of activists or individuals acting alone take action on the basis of communications in newsletters or via the internet. There is no hierarchical organization at all, only a single-level set of like-minded activists tuned to the same network of information. It is a tactic that makes government surveillance and preventive action difficult.[16]

In Europe, too, the rise of right-wing terrorism was the main concern of experts until the events of 11 September 2001 changed the theme. The deadliest right-wing attack in Europe was the bombing of the Bologna railway station on 2 August 1980 that killed 80 people and injured hundreds. It was the work of the neo-fascist *Terza Posizione* (Third Position) organization. Similar neo-Nazi groups carried out less lethal terrorist attacks in Germany at about the same time. Persistent police work reduced right-wing terrorism in Europe for several years, but in the early

1990s skinheads and neo-Nazis in Germany, Austria, France and formerly communist Eastern Europe attacked immigrants and Romas. Groups with racist, anti-immigrant and antigovernment ideologies have become more numerous and more active. Targets include synagogues, mosques, churches, interracial couples, Muslims, Jews, abortion-providers, immigrants, Roma people and gay men. The targets differ from country to country, but Russia, India, Hungary, Britain and the US have all seen numerous attacks. In 1999 alone right-wing extremists bombed a synagogue in Moscow, a black neighborhood in London (Brixton), and the car of an antifascist activist in Sweden.

In some cases the groups that engage in right-wing terror appear to be closely connected with the government or with the military, as the next chapter will discuss. In Guatemala *Mano Blanca* and other death squads targeted people associated in any way with opposition to the government and in Argentina the AAA (Argentine Anti-Communist Alliance) directed its violence against Jews as well as regime opponents.

Left-wing terrorism has declined over the past four decades. Governments had some success in penetrating organizations to learn their plans and in arresting key members. With the end of the Soviet Union a major source of inspiration and support for anti-capitalist causes dried up and the victory of the last anti-colonial struggles changed militants into politicians and administrators. Left-wing political thought no longer had a well-honed analysis that supported a well-defined activist political agenda. Some of the remaining movements, like FARC in Colombia, are still powerful, but they look more and more like political gangs interested in preserving their piece of power. Others, like November 17 in Greece, seem propelled by an inner momentum that has little relation to current realities. Some observers fear that anti-globalization activism and the environmental movement will give rise to terrorist attacks, but there is no indication of any trend in that direction.

How dangerous?

Criminologists have discovered that the level of fear of crime in a society is not very closely related to the actual danger of being a victim of crime. Moreover, police change their definitions of crime and the care with which they record them in response to the urgency expressed by governments and public opinion. Fear of terrorism is like fear of other crimes that affect personal security in this respect. It moves up and down in response to political pronouncements and striking incidents as well as in response to changes in the actual incidence of terrorist acts.

Trackers of terrorism

Before the attacks of 11 September 2001, the trackers of terrorism in the US State Department identified two distinct trends. The first was the long-term decline in the number of terrorist incidents worldwide since a peak in 1987. The other was the rising destructiveness of the attacks that were committed.[17]

Some officials in the administration of President Bill Clinton tried to raise the profile of the danger of terrorism. After the bombing of US embassies in Nairobi and Dar es Salaam in 1998 counter-terrorist activity was expanded, but the public in the US believed that in the universe of terrible dangers – war, natural disaster, ecological breakdown and epidemics – terrorism ranked rather low. The public in other regions, including Europe, also seemed to have learned to live with a level of terrorism, that in most places was declining, without giving the matter much thought. For people in regions especially afflicted by political violence like Israel, Palestine, Colombia and Sri Lanka the issue, of course, remained an urgent concern.

Since the attacks in New York and Washington international terrorism has become an overriding issue for the US Government and many others. There is a concerted effort to keep terrorism at the top of the political agenda. All manner of policy proposals, especially foreign policy, are met with the question: What does it mean for the war on terrorism?

But is the threat really that major? Government officials and think-tank experts believe that terrorist networks are organizing globally and that the sophistication of their communication, planning, training and recruitment has also increased. Moreover, terrorist groups that formerly had localized objectives such as replacing the government in Egypt, Saudi Arabia or Indonesia have joined together in al-Qaeda and added to their separate aims the global goal of damaging the power of the US and its supporters.

Recently the experts signal a huge jump in danger; they point out that it is now technically possible for terrorist groups to initiate a smallpox epidemic, poison the water or the food supply of a large population or explode a device that spreads radiation in a metropolis. The point is made repeatedly: nuclear, biological or chemical (NBC) weapons and anti-US transnational terrorist networks are reason enough for Western governments and their citizens to take terrorism much more seriously.

Some important hard facts support these assessments, but the question of the danger of terrorism is caught in the dilemma of prophesies that may be self-fulfilling. A more lethal arsenal does create new orders of danger, and the growing technical, organizational and financial skill of terrorist groups is real. Equally important, however, is where the new capacities and the motivation to use them come from. How much of the new skill of terrorists derives from training at the hands of the CIA and other forces, often in the name of counter-terrorism? How many of the improved and novel weapons that terrorists might use come from the research labs and the stockpiles of governments? How much do the policies of Western powers contribute to

state breakdown and popular anger that sometimes
turns to terrorist ideologies? In what measure does
President Bush's 'war on terrorism' by its name alone
raise the dignity of terrorists to that of warriors in a
global cause? After taking a closer look at state terrorism and counter-terrorism we will be in a better
position to address some of these questions.

1 Brian Whittaker, *The Guardian*, 4 March 2002. **2** Ann Hansen, *Direct Action: Memoirs of an Urban Guerrilla* (Toronto: Between the Lines, 2001). **3** *The Hindu*, 27 November 2001. **4** *Kuala Lumpur Declaration on International Terrorism*, Session of the Islamic Conference of Foreign Ministers on Terrorism, 1-3 April 2002. **5** Amin Maalouf, *Samarkand* (London: Abacus, 1994), 118. **6** David Rapoport, 'Fear and Trembling: Terrorism in Three Religious Traditions', *American Political Science Review* 78, no. 3 (September 1984): 658-77. **7** Michael Bray, *A Time to Kill: A Study Concerning the Use of Force and Abortion* (Portland, Oregon: Advocates for Life, 1993). **8** Jon Ronson, 'Conspirators', *The Guardian*, 5 May 2002. **9** Rosa Ehrenreich, *The Scars of Death: Children Abducted by the Lord's Resistance Army in Uganda*, Human Rights Watch, New York, 1997. **10** John L Esposito, *Unholy War: Terror in the Name of Islam* (New York: Oxford University Press, 2002), 52-53. **11** Pervez Amir Ali Hoodbhoy, 'How Islam Lost Its Way', *The Washinton Post*, December 30, 2001. **12** Gilles Kepel, 'The Trail of Political Islam', *OpenDemocracy.Net*, 3 July 2002. **13** Ze'ev Schiff and Ehud Yaari, *Intifada: The Palestinian Uprising - Israel's Third Front* (New York: Simon and Schuster, 1989), iv. **14** BBC 28 November 1999. **15** 'Red Brigades', International Policy Institute for Counter-Terrorism (www.ict.org.il) **16** Ely Karmon, 'Right-Wing Terrorism on the Rise', International Policy Institute for Counter-Terrorism, 12 August 1999. **17** US State Department, *Patterns of Global Terrorism-2001*, 21 May 2002.

3 State terrorism

Terrorism always lurks there at the back of the shelf of power tools available to those who command the machinery of government. The agencies and weapons that pursue criminals and wage wars are easily adapted to state-terrorist use. The end of the Cold War saw a decline in both communist and anti-communist state terrorism. However, the new fear of global terrorist networks is stimulating a muscular counter-terrorism that carries dangers of its own.

SOMETIME IN THEIR history most states have conquered new territory and imposed their rule on new populations. In so doing they were using violence against people they aimed to claim as citizens.

State terrorism has an ancient history, but its modern expression is tied to the projection of European state power in acquiring empires in America, Asia and Africa. Spain, Portugal, the Netherlands, Britain, France, Germany, Italy and Japan all used force with frightening moral certainty when they established empires. So did the US in its westward expansion and Russia in its eastward extension. These wars of expansion often included attacks on civilians. One of the first examples of biological terrorism was the deliberate distribution of smallpox-infected blankets to North American Indians.[1]

In places of European settlement, as in the Americas and southern Africa, the indigenous people who resisted the invaders also attacked the new homesteads and settlements. The new settlers, who considered themselves ordinary citizens, appeared to indigenous people as armed thieves threatening their land and game. Fear of such attacks reinforced the military and political drive to clear indigenous people from ancestral lands and either exterminate them or confine them to officially-designated reservations.

The colonial powers continued to use violence to maintain their domination, to recruit labor and soldiers and to seize additional territory for settler farms, mines and other uses. In opening new lands to commercial exploitation colonial governments often ceded political control to private companies. Some of the worst episodes of terror were carried out under the direction of such companies to further their collection

---

Colonial terror

Richard Gott in a review of the Oxford History of the British Empire *recalls some of the state terror that he says the five volumes fail to notice.*

The British [sent] search-and-destroy missions... to Central India in 1817 to slaughter the marauding Pindari armies of Chitu... Colonel George Fitzclarence, an aide-de-camp to the Governor of Bengal... underlined their real purpose. The Pindaris were 'viewed as public robbers', Fitzclarence wrote, and so 'their extirpation was aimed at, and not their defeat as an enemy entitled to the rights of war.'...

[There was a] prolonged campaign to exterminate the San (Bushmen) during the first decades of the 19th century. Hundreds of thousands of acres were seized by white farmers, and hardly a single Bushman band remained by 1825. A correspondent in a frontier town in 1821, describing how he had met people involved in the 'commando' expeditions sent out against them, wrote that 'they talk of shooting Bushmen with the same feelings as if the poor creatures were wild beasts.'...

'How would I civilise the Maoris?' asked Captain John Guard, a former convict whose ship was wrecked off the North Island in 1834. 'Shoot them to be sure! A musket ball for every New Zealander is the only way of civilising their country.'

Colonel William Cox [a wealthy Australian rancher], speaking at a public meeting in Beaufort in 1825: 'The best thing that could be done would be to shoot all the Blacks and manure the ground with their carcasses, which was all the good they were fit for... the women and children should especially be shot as the most certain method of getting rid of the race.' ■

'Shoot them to be sure', *London Review of Books*, 25 April 2002.

Elizabeth Fenn finds state terror in Britain's American colonies.

In 1763... Jeffery Amherst stated his belief that total war against Native Americans was warranted. 'Indeed,' he wrote, 'their Total Extirpation is scarce sufficient Attonement for the Bloody and Inhuman deeds they have Committed.' ■

'Biological Warfare in Eighteenth-Century North America: Beyond Jeffery Amherst', *Journal of American History*, March 2000.

of natural resources. The forced gathering of wild rubber in King Leopold's Congo rivalled in its destructiveness the depredations of the slave trade. Profits from wild rubber were also the incentive for the systematic use of terror to recruit and discipline labor in the forests of the Amazon basin.

Once colonial governments were in place and colonial armies had put down most rebellions, the use of terror decreased, but it did not disappear. Senegalese movie director Ousmane Sembene's film *Emitai* (1971) depicts a historical incident in the French campaign to recruit soldiers and confiscate grain in West African villages for the French war effort in Europe during the Second World War. The women hide the rice and the young men hide in the backlands. The drama descends inevitably into the massacre by colonial police of villagers trying to keep their freedom and conserve their food supply. A few conscience-stricken colonial officials have no way to interrupt the train of events; they are anguished, but implicated. Violence and the threat of violence against civilians who resisted or just inconvenienced colonial governments were a constant theme under colonial rule. New economic and educational opportunities, better-organized government bureaucracies and expanding political rights were arguably positive features of colonialism, but the colonial regimes remained fundamentally despotic, discriminatory and tainted with violence.

Colonial autocracy was not simply the reflex of military expansionists, it was heartily approved by democratic thinkers. John Stuart Mill, England's leading advocate of political liberties, supported colonial autocracy as a kind of benevolent despotism that would bring backward people to the level of education and enlightenment he saw as preconditions for democratic citizenship. His French friend, Alexis de Tocqueville, shortly after publishing the second volume of his famous *Democracy in America*, turned into a vociferous supporter of terrorist tactics in the French conquest and 'pacification' of Algeria. In the 1840s as Deputy in the National Assembly he gave personal backing to General Thomas Bugeaud whose brutal methods in Algeria were receiving criticism at the time. Returning from a visit there in October 1841, de Tocqueville wrote: 'In France I have often heard people I respect, but do not approve, deplore burning harvests, emptying granaries and seizing unarmed men, women and children. As I see it, these are unfortunate necessities that any people wishing to make war on the Arabs must accept... I believe the laws of war entitle us to ravage the country and that we must do this, either by destroying crops at harvest time, or all the time by making rapid incursions, known as raids, the aim of which is to carry off men and flocks.'[2]

Other European liberals and democrats were, like de Tocqueville, motivated to defend national honor and the military virtues of discipline and loyalty and to give political expression to their belief in the cultural or racial superiority of Europeans. Few were as frank as de Tocqueville in supporting state terrorism in the colonial projects that implemented their beliefs, perhaps because the argument so blatantly contradicts the principle of human equality. Later architects of state terrorism found other ways to justify their actions.

Perfecting state terrorism

The most notorious cases of terrorism by governments against their own citizens are those of Nazi Germany and the Soviet Union under Joseph Stalin. Special police pursued groups deemed unreliable or unwanted with unprecedented efficiency and ruthlessness. These regimes made political conformity a central ideological tenet to be accomplished by any means necessary, including terror. They targeted particular categories of their citizens for physical elimination. They made terrorism a core method for enforcing control over the minds and actions of their subjects.

They were successful for many years in keeping citizens frightened and off-balance, and eliminating individuals and groups that might have organized an opposition.

One local study gives a striking portrait of how Nazi terror worked. In the town of Thalburg the Nazi party seized local power in a series of steps over a period of about six months after Hitler was named Chancellor of Germany in 1933. Under Nazi control, the police, with the support of locally organized gangs of Brownshirts, used unpredictable arrests, house searches and intimidation to spread fear and uncertainty among the population. Once the local Nazi party gained control of the local government its leadership could remove all opposition party members from government roles and government jobs. Nazi party loyalists took control of every sports club and civic association in the town, not all at once, but one at a time.

According to a theory popular today such associations play a vital role supporting democratic beliefs and practices.[3] On that view the numerous associations in Thalburg should have been centers of resistance to the Nazi takeover. That they were not attests to the efficacy of well-orchestrated state terror. There was no point at which organized opponents could gather their strength and say 'now we must resist.' Instead they were isolated and left not only disorganized, but lonely and fearful. Potential organizers were neutralized, sent to concentration camps or driven into exile.

The Nazis took control of all the newspapers and shaped the news coverage to their liking. They turned the schools to the teaching of national socialist doctrines, including anti-semitism. Ceremony, ritual and the media outlets kept up a drumbeat of support for Hitler, the local Nazis and Nazi doctrine. After several months the system of terror became routinized and the open use of brutal violence was no longer necessary. On the larger canvas ugly and open violence did not cease; terrorism, war and exterminism marked the evolution of the Third Reich.

The Soviet Union under Stalin systematized the use of terror even before Hitler did in Germany. Stalin met the widespread resistance to collectivization of agriculture in the early 1930s with arrests, torture and forced labor. The network of forced labor camps received another wave of prisoners in the late 1930s as officials forced the pace of collectivization. The great purges of the leadership of the Communist Party and the military officer corps visited terrorism upon holders of power and influence who might have stood in the way of Stalin and his policies of centralization and crash industrialization. The famous show trials with the dramatic confessions of former heroes were only the most publicized part of a system of terror that targeted political and industrial managers, artists, intellectuals and academics who could be removed from their jobs, sent to prison camps or simply killed.

Estimates vary widely, but it seems that at least 10 million citizens were sent to forced labor camps in the 1930s and 1940s. Prisoners were forced to live and to work under atrocious conditions. After Stalin's death in 1953 the population of the labor camps declined and most were disbanded in 1956. Over the whole course of the camps' existence millions died, many of them executed. The terror was calculated to keep all possible critics off-balance, fearful, isolated and helpless. As in the town of Thalburg in Hitler's Germany the active use of terror in the USSR gradually declined and became an institutionalized feature of the dictatorship.

The national security state

In the 1970s several Latin American countries adopted a model of government that came to be called the national security state. The military rulers focused all the powers of the state against the forces of 'communism' and social reformism which they believed were destabilizing influences that threatened the geopolitical integrity of the nation. Their key instruments were police and military forces which, together with semi-autonomous right-wing death squads, used terror against the population at large and groups they regarded as politically suspect. After the military coup against Salvador Allende in 1973 in Chile that brought General Augusto Pinochet to power, the Government rounded up a wide spectrum of possible opponents and killed over 3,000 people. In Argentina the campaign of mothers to find out what happened to their sons and daughters, among the 13,000 to 15,000 people who were 'disappeared' under the military government that ruled from 1976 to 1983, has continued for two decades.

US support was instrumental in fostering the rise to power of the national security regimes in Latin America. From Brazil in 1964 to Central America in the 1980s the US gave more than general diplomatic support; it contributed to the nuts and bolts of the security agenda by training soldiers and police. Some 60,000 Latin American soldiers attended courses at the most prominent of several training facilities, the School of the Americas (in Panama from 1946 to 1984 and at Fort Benning, Georgia since then). Training manuals used in courses covered methods of political control and interrogation that included assassination and torture.[4]

The School gained notoriety when a US Congressional investigation of the murder in El Salvador of six priests, their housekeeper and her daughters discovered that 19 of the 26 soldiers held responsible for the killings had been trained at the School. Under pressure from protests the US Government declassified key documents that

brought to light a roll call of senior alumni which read like a who's who of the most brutal military dictators and human-rights violators in Latin America over the past five decades: Manuel Noriega and Omar Torrijos of Panama; Anastasio Somoza of Nicaragua; Leopoldo Galtieri of Argentina; Generals Hector Gramajo and

Manuel Antonio Callejas of Guatemala; Hugo Banzer Suarez of Bolivia; the El Salvador death-squad leader Roberto D'Aubuisson. A more detailed examination of the declassified lists reveals that more than 500 soldiers who had received training at the academy have since been held responsible for some of the most hideous atrocities carried out in countries in the region during the years they were racked by civil wars and since.[5]

In response to congressional criticism and efforts to close the School its name was changed in 2001 to the Western Hemisphere Institute for Security Cooperation (WHISC).

Arsenals of repression

The communist, Nazi and national security states that have adopted terrorism against their own citizens as a routine instrument of rule put forward elaborate ideological justifications for their use of violence and fear. Terrorism was not an unconscious reflex. The ideology generally claimed that evil, deceitful and violent enemies of the *volk*, the party or the state were secretly working to undermine and destroy what the government was dedicated to defending. Whether the enemies were Jews, capitalist roaders, communists, *kulaks*, subversives or urban guerrillas they deserved to be treated with contempt, coercion and liquidation.

Each ideology had its own specific mix of terrorist measures. Invasive and unpredictable searches, arbitrary arrests, torture, imprisonment in special camps, threats to family and deprivation of employment – all seem to be common elements in the arsenal of state terrorist methods. Other methods were more specific to particular ideologies: extermination of Jews, Romas and homosexuals in purpose-designed death camps with gas chambers were a Nazi invention; show trials, land seizures and deliberate starvation were specialities of Stalinism; death squads, torture cells and dropping victims from aircraft into the sea were prominent features of the national security states of Latin America.

Several governments in recent years have used terrorist action against particular ethnic groups. The military government of Myanmar (Burma) has since 1962 used violence against ethnic minorities, particularly the Shan, Karen, Karenni and Rohingya groups. In his report for the year 2000 UN special investigator Rajsoomer Lallah cited summary executions as well as 'extortion, rape, torture, forced labor and portering' (forced carrying of heavy loads). He reported that women were often the victims of these violations. This ongoing use of state terrorism has continued for decades alongside the repression of the National League for Democracy led by Aung San Suu Kyi – the party never allowed to take office after it won the 1990 elections.[6] Under President Suharto, Indonesia's murderous 25-year repression in East Timor killed an estimated 200,000 people, one quarter of the population. The terror was reignited after the East Timorese voted for independence in August 1999 and thousands more were killed in well-planned massacres.

The most notorious recent cases of state terrorism aimed at exterminating a section of a country's population are those of Cambodia and Rwanda. The Cambodian Communist Party or Khmer Rouge, a revolutionary movement led by Pol Pot, gained power in Cambodia after the terrible destruction and disorganization brought about by the US destabilization campaign in Cambodia from 1969 to 1973 with its intensive, secret and illegal bombing. Between 1975 and 1978 the Pol Pot regime turned all its efforts to constructing a purified Khmer rural society. It forced the urban population to move to the countryside and executed at least 200,000 people, many of them deemed to be contaminated with imperialism or Vietnamese blood or culture. Intellectuals, professionals, civil servants and cultural leaders were systematically eliminated. Forced labor on construction and agricultural schemes, starvation and disease killed another 1.5 million Cambodians. About one

Cambodian in five was exterminated. The Government's ruthless hold on power continued until it was driven from office by the Vietnamese invasion of 1979.[7]

The genocidal state terrorism in Rwanda in 1994 was another case of the 'deliberate choice of a modern élite to foster hatred and fear to keep itself in power' and, it must be added, to fulfill a political program. While the program of the Khmer Rouge was influenced by Marxism-Leninism and Maoism as well as by Khmer racism, the program of the group that gained control of the interim government of Rwanda was simply to kill as many of the Tutsi minority as they could and to reconfigure the country according to mythical ideas of an ancient and pure Hutu society. The Hutu-dominated government was faced with a growing guerrilla opposition led by the Rwanda Patriotic Front (RPF), whose core leadership came from the Tutsis who had become refugees in Uganda. In 1993 Hutu leaders around President Juvenal Habyarimana, including some intellectuals and military officers, began to plan for the systematic killing of Tutsis. One important instrument was to be a youth militia, the *Interahamwe*, that already existed and had begun to attack Tutsis. Another scheme was to form a 'civilian defense force' separate from government that could act rapidly when the signal to start killing came.

The opportunity to unleash the plan arrived on 6 April 1994 when persons still unknown shot down the plane in which President Habyarimana was returning from peace negotiations. The group around the President who had planned the extermination decided to act. The first step was to kill government and opposition leaders, mainly Hutu, who were not part of the plan in order to create a power vacuum. Colonel Bagosora and his Presidential Guard took the lead in this operation. He became the leader of the interim government that directed the rapidly-expanding waves of killing. The guns and grenades of the militia and the army were crucial, but the leaders found the killing could be speeded up by enlisting popular groups using machetes and other hand-powered weapons. Gangs moving house to house were less effective than forcing or tricking targeted people to gather in a church or school where they could be burned, shot or slashed to death. Radio was used to orchestrate the process and participation was encouraged with promises of access to the land and houses of the victims and by threats of punishment. There are well-documented reports that those leading the operations gave orders to the killers to degrade, mutilate and rape the women they were about to murder.

Over time the genocide planners were able to enlist much of the state apparatus in the killing. Resistors were eliminated. As remarkable as the collaboration of military officers and professional administrators was the absence of any effective international action to halt the killings. In thirteen weeks about 500,000 people, three-quarters of the Tutsi population, were killed. Over time the genocide ceased to give the interim government internal cohesion or win popular support. International disapproval finally began to hurt it, but it was the military success of the RPF that brought the regime and its program of genocide to an end.[8]

Episodes of state terrorism

Many governments have made less wholehearted use of terrorism. The organizational chart of most existing governments hides some agency with a terrorism brief and the state's history conceals some episode in which state terrorism became a prominent feature of politics. In France long before the revolutionary state's Great Terror in which successive leaders of the revolution sent one another to the guillotine, the Roman Catholic establishment waged a campaign in the 11th century against the Cathars in south-western France who stood against the Roman church and the corruption of the clergy. Northern French nobility backed the church in a crusade against the resisting heretics. The Treaty of

Paris confirmed the subordination of the southern nobility that had harbored the Cathars (see p 74), but it failed to root out the movement, despite the massacre of many of its followers. It took the systematic terrorism of the Inquisition in the 13th and 14th centuries with its reliance on informants, searches of homes, harsh questioning and torture to extinguish the 'heresy'.

In the United States the defeated plantocracy after the civil war used terror to re-establish its dominance and to disempower former slaves. Under the slave system the private property privileges of slave owners had kept the essential violence of the slave system largely in the private realm. After the civil war former slave owners founded the Ku Klux Klan (KKK) to resist the changes in the social hierarchy pursued in Reconstruction. In North Carolina, Tennessee and Georgia, the KKK played a large part in restoring the political dominance of the white élite. The white élite kept the newly enfranchised African-American ex-slaves from entering the public sphere of politics through a combination of terrorism and restrictive legislation. The Ku Klux Klan was the main terrorist instrument of the local interests that controlled state governments. Its secret meetings, rituals and cross burnings were designed to frighten, but it was murder, violence and direct intimidation that made it effective. The intimidation backed up the Jim Crow legislation (segregation in public places, poll taxes, literacy tests for voting) that disenfranchised and disempowered African-Americans.

States often use Klan-like proxy organizations to carry out terrorism against the state's own citizens. The apartheid government in South Africa, for example, in one of many state terrorist operations ordered 'hit squads' associated with Chief Buthelezi's Inkatha party to attack members of the African National Congress.[9] Frequently parts of the government do not support such actions and may not know about them. In the US the federal government focussed enough opposition to the terrorism of the KKK to legislate restrictions that reduced its effectiveness.

Behind the exclusionary ideology and the attraction to terrorist violence expressed in all these examples of state terrorism lies a profound cynicism about popular politics. Hitler put it most concisely: 'Cruelty impresses. Cruelty and raw force. The simple man in the street is impressed only by brute force and ruthlessness. Terror is the most effective political means.' It is a political means that poisons the normal politics of debate, negotiation and confrontation.

Transnational state terrorism

Another variety of state terrorism is government-sponsored acts of violence across borders to harm, kill and intimidate civilians of another country. The term 'terrorist state' as it is used in the press and by governments usually refers to this kind of terrorism. Although governments bent on troubling other states or movements in other countries sometimes act through official government agencies, they usually prefer to act through proxy organizations, sometimes called 'cutouts', and to keep their own role invisible.

The aim of transnational state terrorism may be to destabilize and weaken a government that is perceived to be hostile and perhaps a supporter of groups regarded as terrorist opponents. The accusations, and at times the reality, of terrorism are flung in both directions. Apartheid South Africa went to great lengths to counter the popular movements for decolonization in southern Africa. As Angola and Mozambique moved toward independence, apartheid South Africa made extensive use of terror (as well as outright warfare) to keep the newly independent governments weak and disorganized. Their 'total strategy' of defense was similar to the pattern of the national security states of South America. In 1976 their armed forces took over support for Renamo (*Resistencia Nacional Mocambicana*), the terrorist opposition to the new government in Mozambique formed by Frelimo (Front for the Liberation of Mozambique). Renamo had been nurtured by the Rhodesian security forces, who had recruited dissident Frelimo fighters to destabilize the new Frelimo government. Renamo became infamous for the brutality of its attacks on civilians and for its targeting of schools and health clinics as well as economic installations like roads, electric lines and pipelines.

A pattern of reciprocal violence that includes terrorism sometimes repeats itself in the relations between hostile neighboring countries. Each government supports terrorist or guerrilla operations inside its rival. India and Pakistan repeatedly accuse each other of terrorism in the disputed territory of Kashmir.

Inquisition

In 1208 the Albigensian Crusade was launched by Pope Innocent III – a Crusade which was to accomplish the destruction of the remarkable culture which nurtured this 'heresy.' Had this culture, which fostered tolerance of Jews and Muslims, respect for women and women priests, the appreciation of poetry, music and beauty, been allowed to survive and thrive, it is possible that Europe might have been spared its wars of religion, its witch-hunts and its holocausts of victims sacrificed in later centuries to religious and ideological bigotry.

In 1216 the Dominican Order was established to counter the teaching of the popular Cathar priesthood. However, in 1233 a Papal Bull conferred on the Order the task of eradicating heresy and it then became the main vehicle of the Inquisition, given authority over and above local Catholic bishops to convict suspected heretics without any possibility of appeal. The Dominicans set up an efficient machinery for the 'process of the investigation, indictment, trial, torture and execution of heretics.' Inquisitors were granted the right to expropriate the entire property of heretics. Even the bodies of the dead suspected of heresy were dug up and burnt. At first the Dominicans were not permitted to administer torture themselves but from 1252 they were given Papal permission to do so although they still handed over their victims to the civil authorities for execution. Victims could be tortured twice a day for a week or more by methods which assiduously avoided the shedding of blood but maximised the degree of pain and terror inflicted until a confession of guilt was obtained. Again, to avoid the shedding of blood, death by burning at the stake was the preferred method of 'extermination.' ∎

Anne Baring, *Review of Michael Baigent and Richard Leigh, The Inquisition* (Viking, New York: 1999), www.womenpriests.org

In the Middle East, support for Palestinian groups that engage in terrorism in Israel comes from Saudi Arabia, Syria, Iraq and Iran. The Government of Israel claims that the Palestinian Authority, a quasi-state, is responsible for many of the suicide bombings of civilian gatherings in Israel claimed by Hamas, Islamic Jihad, Tanzim and the al-Aqsa Martyrs' Brigade. On its side the Israeli Government has sent its defense forces to assassinate people it claims are responsible for terrorism and it has militarized its occupation of Palestinian settlements and refugee camps in the West Bank. In these operations its forces have killed many civilians.

The Cold War and containment

The Cold War generated widely spread reciprocal support for rival terrorisms from the United States and the Soviet Union. The two superpowers were drawn to almost every conflict in the world if only to ensure that the other side did not gain some advantage from it. In all the conflicts mentioned above one can find US or Soviet fingerprints somewhere along the way. The superpowers gave important direct and indirect support to organizations that made extensive use of terrorism, including training them in terrorist techniques. The scale of superpower involvement in terrorism gives the lie to the common view that terrorism is exclusively 'the weapon of the weak'. Often it is the weapon with which the strong get the weak to do their dirty work for them.

In its preoccupation with containing communism, the US saw danger in the decolonizing world and in many other places besides. President John Kennedy's government initiated a long-running effort to bring down the Castro regime. After the failed Bay of Pigs invasion in 1961, US-trained anti-Castro Cubans repeatedly committed acts of violence against Cuba. As recently as the mid 1990s they planted bombs designed to cripple the growing Cuban tourist industry.[10] (The same groups have been convicted of attacks in Miami against Cubans doing business with Cuba.[11])

In the 1980s the Reagan administration sounded the alarm about a 'terror network' orchestrated by the Soviet Union threatening US and Western interests around the globe and especially in southern Africa, Central America, the Middle East and Central Asia. Fear of instability and distrust of nationalist regimes and movements drew the US to embrace governments that abused human rights, to support agencies that engaged in terrorism and to sponsor certain terrorist activities of its own. In Angola, Nicaragua, Afghanistan and Kampuchea (Cambodia) the US supported, and sometimes created, insurgencies that they tried to present as democratic and freedom-seeking. Often these groups practiced terrorism.

The Soviet Union was not squeamish about supporting violence, but most anti-colonial movements were largely peaceful and those that engaged in violence, even those professing Marxism and receiving Soviet support gravitated to guerrilla warfare and directed their arms at military and police targets. Some, like the African National Congress in South Africa committed occasional acts of terrorism.

The Soviets did support governments that engaged in state terrorism including those of Muammar al-Qaddafi in Libya and Mengistu Haile Mariam in Ethiopia. Other communist governments, including those in Cuba, Cambodia, North Vietnam, Eastern Europe and China made use of terrorism in consolidating and retaining political control. No doubt the example of Stalinism played a part in choosing purges, assassinations and imprisonment over negotiation and accommodation.

Overthrow

In 1953 and 1954 the US Government through the CIA engineered the overthrow of nationalist and reformist governments in Iran and Guatemala and the installation of regimes that used terrorism to weaken and control political opposition and drive local communist parties underground. In preparation for these operations of 'regime change' the CIA gathered detailed intelligence about potential friends and foes, disseminated propaganda in the form of leaflets, manipulated news reports to encourage opposition and concocted evidence of Soviet involvement. The agency also identified alternative rulers and induced them to take action, promising financial and diplomatic backing to a new government.[12] In 1953 the CIA with Britain's Secret Intelligence Service (SIS) spearheaded the coup against Prime Minister Mohammad Mossadegh of Iran to counter his nationalization of the British Petroleum Company and to move against the communist Tudeh party whose influence they feared was growing. They readily identified General Fazlollah Zahedi as a replacement leader. After several false moves they induced the Shah to abandon his original indifference to politics and to support the change in government. To foment street demonstrations CIA agents posing as communists threatened Muslim clerics with 'savage punishment if they opposed Mossadegh' and bombed the home of a prominent Muslim. These were two measures of direct terrorism committed by US agencies.[13]

In 1954 the US followed a similar plan in Guatemala. After an intense public relations campaign financed by the United Fruit Company (in which Secretary of State John Foster Dulles and CIA Director Allen Dulles had personal financial interest) President Eisenhower approved another project of regime change. The CIA took the lead in organizing a dissident army to invade from neighboring Honduras to overthrow the government of Jacabo Arbenz whose policies of land reform, higher corporate taxes and university education for lower-class youth troubled the United Fruit Company and the established élite. The two groups also worried that the influence of communism in Guatemala would grow. The US provided air cover for the invasion and the CIA mounted a large disinformation campaign exaggerating the size and effectiveness of the invasion. There was some US-sponsored violence in Guatemala: boarding peaceful vessels off the coast and bombing a few targets inside the country.[14]

In both these cases the real link to terror came after the coup when the replacement regimes arrested, tortured and killed opponents and dissidents. The CIA helped train the security forces of the new governments and maintained close ongoing relations with them. Iran's State Intelligence and Security Organization, known as SAVAK, became famous for the long reach of its agents who hunted down regime opponents around the world. In the US alone it used 13 case-officers to keep track of some 30,000 Iranian students. SAVAK was established in 1957 with the guidance of US and Israeli intelligence services. It first sought to arrest members of the Tudeh party, but it grew into a full-scale secret police operation with high tech equipment from the US to monitor and collate information on all aspects of political and civic activity. It kept newspapers, journalists, labor unions, peasants' organizations and other civic associations under tight surveillance. It established its own prisons and made extensive use of brutal methods of torture. Observers estimate that in response to the demonstrations of 1978, SAVAK killed 13,000 to 15,000 Iranian citizens and seriously injured another 50,000.[15] Throughout its existence the CIA remained its close collaborator.

A detailed CIA study of the Iran coup draws as one lesson that the CIA's military planners have political arrest lists ready.[16] In Guatemala they certainly had such a list for what the CIA planning document called 'the roll-up of Communists and collaborators'. After the coup the police rounded up and killed hundreds of people. A system of deadly repression making extensive use of death squads dressed as civilians, but taking orders from security forces, was put in place. The resistance, weak as it was, of indigenous peoples and the obligation to fight communism were the repeated excuses for a reign of terror that killed some 100,000 Guatemalans over the next four decades. The US remained a close and supportive partner of the government of Guatemala through most of these years, giving assistance in designing and setting up an urban counter-terrorist task force and in supplying military advisers and equipment.[17]

Government terror

The record shows that government terror and killing of Mayan villagers in Guatemala peaked in the early 1980s just when the US was pumping up its overt and clandestine campaign to overthrow the Nicaraguan government of the *Frente Sandinista de Liberación National* (FSLN or Sandinistas) that had gained power in 1979 when the US-supported military apparatus of dictator Anastasio Somoza collapsed. President Ronald Reagan's government was fearful of what they considered to be expanding communist influence in Central America and the Caribbean and especially vexed by the successful guerrilla war of the left-wing Sandinista movement. Policy planners centered in the National Security Agency and the CIA put into practice the doctrine of 'low intensity warfare' to force the replacement of the Sandinistas by a conservative and pliant set of rulers.

At the heart of the method was the creation of a guerrilla army out of members of Somoza's National Guard and several other splinter groups revolving around Eden Pastora, a dissident former Sandinista. Documents recently released under the Freedom of Information Act show that the Contras, as the grouping was known, were wholly created and controlled by the US. The Contras were instructed to hit 'soft targets' like agricultural cooperatives and some of them were advised by US experts and manuals about 'how to use selective violence' and 'coercive counter-intelligence interrogation of resistant sources'. The Contras often attacked civilians, even rounded them up and shot them.

In order to make the Contras look more effective than they were and to cripple the economy of Nicaragua the US conducted direct military operations, attacking economic targets like oil depots and allowing the Contras to take the credit. To back up the impression that the Contras were an indigenous reality the US mounted a sophisticated public relations and news-generating effort. President Reagan uttered his famous

Algeria

The polarized debate today over the ethics of suicide bombing in Israel uncannily recalls a similar debate in France in the 1950s. At that time, Albert Camus broke with fellow existentialist Jean-Paul Sartre – a fierce opponent of French colonialism – to condemn the use of indiscriminate violence on both sides, French and Algerian. The moral symmetry of Camus's plea was admirable. But as Sartre pointed out, it rested on a faulty political logic. For what makes oppression so tragic is precisely that it often forces the oppressed to adopt methods as brutal as those of their oppressors, in order to win their share of human freedom.

Late in Gillo Pontecorvo's popular, neo-realist film, 'The Battle of Algiers' (1967), which unflinchingly chronicles the guerilla war, a scene occurs in which Ben H'midi, the captured political leader of the FLN, is asked by a French journalist how he could justify murdering innocent French civilians. In a reference to the French use of napalm and carpet-bombing in the countryside, H'midi replies: 'Let us have your bombers and you can have our women's baskets.'

France's campaign in Algiers instantly became a classic of counter-insurgency warfare. To break the FLN's network, French paratroopers cordoned off the Casbah and rounded up thousands of Algerian men (without charge). The French tortured and executed (without trial) thousands of young Algerian men and women. Eventually, such ruthless tactics worked. The French smashed the network of urban guerilla cells...

Algeria achieved its independence in 1962... Twenty thousand French died uselessly to preserve the colony. One million Algerians died for their freedom. ■

John Sanbonmatsu, *Will the Battle for Jerusalem Become the Battle of Algiers? Suicide Bombings and Colonialism - Then and Now*, April 2002, http://opgreens.org

comparison: the Contras are 'the moral equivalent of our founding fathers'. The Atlantic and Caribbean ports of Nicaragua were mined by the US with the goal of raising the costs of marine insurance high enough to strangle Nicaragua's vital seaborne trade.

The US has had a role in overthrowing several other governments on the grounds of their unreliability in the Cold War alignment. The assassination of Patrice Lumumba in the Congo in 1961 and the installation of Joseph Mobutu as President, inaugurated a cycle of corrupt and tyrannical government. The change from Sukarno to Suharto in Indonesia in 1965 precipitated mass killings of 500,000 to 1,000,000 people. To clear the way for the coup d'état against Salvador Allende's government in Chile in 1973 the CIA worked actively with members of the Chilean military to 'neutralize' General Rene Schneider, Commander-in-Chief of the Chilean Army. Schneider was a strong constitutionalist known to oppose a coup against the legally elected President. When a group of officers with whom the CIA had been collaborating killed General Schneider in 1970, the US assisted in protecting the assassins.[18] It was the first political assassination in Chile since 1837.

Changes of government are usually complex events and the interventions are clandestine and may come from more than one country. The interveners try to make use of local social and military forces that have a life of their own. The terrorist element in the US role in these coups seems often to have been that of an accomplice – supplying encouragement, money and weapons, assurance of future support and a list of dangerous individuals and organizations.

More telling is the continued involvement of the US military and security specialists, assisting the design and organization of a security apparatus and the training of people in the skills of interrogation and 'counter-insurgency' operations. US officials know full well that such an apparatus and the skills learned are often turned to the systematic and long-term employment of terror to keep a government in power.

'Blowback' and instability

From the standpoint of the US strategists there are two big dangers: 'blowback' and instability. Blowback is the CIA term for the unintended, unforeseen and unwanted consequences of secret operations. It is used frequently to describe the actions of organizations that the US created and strengthened that later turn against US-related targets. One kind of blowback is terrorism against US interests. The US invested money, training and equipment to make the Taliban and other fundamentalist groups in Pakistan and Afghanistan

---

Training for terror

The CIA used two secret manuals... to train Latin American militaries and security services in interrogating suspects, one titled 'KUBARK Counterintelligence Interrogation – July 1963,' and an updated version titled 'Human Resource Exploitation Training Manual -1983.' These two documents were declassified in January 1997 in response to a 1994 Freedom of Information Act request by the *Baltimore Sun*, and the *Sun*'s threat of a lawsuit under FOIA. The *Sun* headlined its report on the documents (27 January 1997, by Gary Cohn, Ginger Thompson, and Mark Matthews) as 'Torture was taught by CIA.' The *Sun*'s story noted the admonition on page 46 of the 1963 manual that when planning an interrogation room, 'the electric current should be known in advance, so that transformers or other modifying devices will be on hand if needed.' The *Sun* reported that '...this referred to the application of electric shocks to interrogation suspects.'

The 1963 manual included a 22-page section titled 'The Coercive Counterintelligence Interrogation of Resistant Sources,' which on page 100 admonishes that 'drugs (and the other aids discussed in this section) should not be used persistently to facilitate the interrogative debriefing that follows capitulation. Their function is to cause capitulation, to aid in the shift from resistance to cooperation. Once this shift has been accomplished, coercive techniques should be abandoned both for moral reasons and because they are unnecessary and even counter-productive.' ∎

Tom Blanton, *The CIA in Latin America*. National Security Archive Electronic Briefing Book No. 27. ~http://www.gwu.edu/~nsarchiv

---

effective fighters against Soviet domination of Afghanistan. The Soviets were driven out and the Soviet regime was weakened. Regime change in favor of the Taliban brought stability to a chronically unstable land. But when men trained at the Taliban's schools planted bombs in Saudi Arabia and Egypt critics saw blowback. In targeting governments allied with the US the fighters formerly serving Western interests in the Cold War re-emerged as anti-Western terrorists. With Taliban support for al-Qaeda the blowback continued.

The possibility of instability can also promote terrorism. The strategy of inducing regime change by intervening covertly to support a coup usually assumes that a freshly-formed military government willing to use well-structured security methods can control political forces and stay in power. Factional fights, inexperience and regional tensions make stability a rare commodity. The support for Lon Nol's coup against the mercurial Prince Sihanouk in Cambodia in 1970 is a good example – a search for stability contributing to repression and backlash. The US interest in stability pushes it to give increasing support to those who control the repressive apparatus in the new government and to condone, if not deliberately enhance, its reliance on state terror.

State terrorism after the Cold War

For the four decades after the Second World War, US state terrorism and support for states that engaged in state terrorism was tied to the Cold War and the strategy of containment. Since the end of the Cold War many dictatorships have been replaced by elected governments (Southern Cone of South America, Central America, South Africa, Indonesia). The reasons for these changes include the strength and skill of popular movements and the reduction of US support for repressive governments. Similarly on the other side of the Cold War the break-up of the Soviet Union and the end of Soviet control over Eastern Europe removed a pattern of Soviet-supported state terrorism in some 20 countries from East Germany to Kyrgyzstan.

Yet state terrorism remains a reality and a potential. The genocide in Rwanda, the violence of Robert Mugabe's government in Zimbabwe against the legal opposition and the actions of Russia in Chechnya show that state terrorism has causes beyond the Cold War. The US may be less prone to support terrorist states than in the days of the Cold War, but the attacks in New York and Washington raise a new possibility. Under the influence of the war on terrorism and the idea that 'those not with us are against us' the US may support 'friendly' governments that engage in state

Government arms vs al-Qaeda arms

From the following story it seems that al-Qaeda has at most about $200 million a year to finance its operations. Half of that, $100 million, may be for its military operations. Comparing that with the government military spending figures given below, the ratio of al-Qaeda's weapons to the weapons of governments ranges from about 1:4000 for the US to 1:6 for Sudan.

UNITED NATIONS: Citing unidentified government sources and experts on terrorism, the report said that ostensibly legitimate business continued to be managed on behalf of al-Qaeda across North Africa, the Middle East, Europe and Asia, estimated to be worth $30 million, with some saying as high as $300 million. Without giving names, the report said al-Qaeda had investments in Mauritius, Singapore, Malaysia, the Philippines and Panama and undefined bank accounts in Dubai, Hong Kong, London, Malaysia and Vienna. It contended that private donations to al-Qaeda from wealthy supporters, estimated at up to $156 million a year, were believed to 'continue, largely unabated.' ∎

Evelyn Leopold, Reuters, 29 August 2002.

According to the Center for Defense Information, military expenditure in selected countries was as follows in the year 2000.

US	$396 billion	Turkey	$5 billion
Russia	$60 billion	Pakistan	$3 billion
Saudi Arabia	$27 billion	Colombia	$2 billion
India	$16 billion	Philippines	$1 billion
Israel	$9 billion	Cuba	$0.7 billion
Spain	$7 billion	Sudan	$0.6 billion

terrorist campaigns against their own or the citizens of neighboring countries. Russia (Chechnya), Pakistan (Kashmir), Uzbekistan, Tajikistan and Kyrgyzstan all seem to fit this pattern.[19]

The possibility that the US is still willing to give support to governments and groups that make extensive use of terrorism raises a deeper question. Was it a Cold War dynamic, no longer operative, that drew the US and the West into supporting terrorist regimes or was it defense of the West's global economic and resource interests? Anti-communism or imperialism? And could the new global manicheanism of good democrats vs evil terrorists be a conscious effort to reconstruct a doctrinal defense of support for governments and policies that favor the corporate global economic agenda even if they repress genuinely popular movements? Will other governments such as Russia use a similar logic and support governments within their historic sphere of influence that engage in terrorism?

The amount of state terrorist activity and its continuing appeal is not surprising given the huge concentration of control over weapons that governments enjoy. Criminal gangs, terrorist organizations, guerrilla armies, private businesses and individuals may own many guns and a lot of explosives. Yet their arms are dwarfed by the firepower at the disposal of governments. Furthermore, governments have a huge stake in protecting their political power from rivals and enemies. It is little wonder that government leaders can be tempted to use terrorism to translate the money, arms and intelligence at their disposal into enhancement of their grip on power and their capacity to pursue other political aims.

Perhaps the surprising thing is that governments are not more prone to terrorism than they are. The frequency of deleterious 'blowback' may deter some leaders. Certainly political action in defense of civil liberties and in favor of full disclosure of government action can help discourage government leaders from

terrorist temptation and strengthen the hold of a culture of open political encounter.

1 Elizabeth A Fenn, 'Biological Warfare in Eighteenth-Century North America:
Beyond Jeffery Amherst**,'** *Journal of American History* 86, no. 4 (March 2000):
1554-58. **2** Olivier Le Cour Grandmaison, 'Liberty, equality and colony', *Le
Monde Diplomatique* 11 July 2001. **3** Robert Putnam, 'Bowling Alone,'
Journal of Democracy 6, no. 1 (January 1995). **4** Robert Parry, 'Lost History:
'Project X' and School of Assassins', The Consortium of Independent
Journalism (www.consortiumnews.com). **5** Christine Toomey, 'The Killing
Fields', *Sunday Times Magazine*, 18 November 2001. **6** Rajsoomer Lallah,
Situation of Human Rights in Myanmar (United Nations Economic and Social
Council, Commission on Human Rights, 2000). **7** Ben Kiernan, *The Pol Pot
Regime: Race, Power, and Genocide in Cambodia Under the Khmer Rouge,
1975-79* (New Haven: Yale University Press, 1996). **8** Human Rights Watch,
Leave None to Tell the Story: Genocide in Rwanda (1999). **9** Norm Dixon,
'New evidence: apartheid terror ordered from the top', *Green Left Weekly*, no.
344 (9 June 1996). **10** Saul Landau, 'A Double Standard on Terrorism', *In
These Times*, 4 March 2002. **11** US Department of Justice, Federal Bureau of
Investigation,'Cuban Anti-Castro Terrorism', Washington DC 20535, 16 May
1990. **12** William Blum, *The CIA: A Forgotten History* (London: Zed Books,
1986). **13** 'The CIA in Iran', *The New York Times on the Web*
(www.nytimes.com/library/world/mideast/041600iran-cia-chapter2.html).
14 William Blum, *The CIA: A Forgotten History* (London: Zed Books, 1986).
15 Federation of American Scientists (www.fas.org). **16** Donald N Wilber,
*Clandestine Service History: The Overthrow of Premier Mossadeq of Iran
November 1952-August 1953* (Washington, DC: CIA, 1969), Appendix E:
Military Critique – Lessons Learned from TPAJX re Military Planning Aspects
of Coup d'Etat, p. 19. **17** National Security Archive Electronic Briefing Book
No. 11, US Policy in Guatemala, 1966-1996 (www.gwu.edu/~nsarchiv).
18 US government, 'CIA Activities in Chile', September 18 2000**.**
(www.cia.gov/cia/publications/chile/#15). **19** Ahmed Rashid, 'They're Only
Sleeping', *The New Yorker*, 11 February 2002.

4 Morality and history

Since President Bush's declaration of war on terrorism, in just about every country in the world there has been an explosion of speeches, meetings, publications, laws and cartoons about terrorism. There is a clear attempt to shape people's thinking and gain their support for action of one kind or another. A map of the moral and historical arguments that opinion-shapers deploy is useful for developing one's own independent viewpoint.

THE LOUDEST AND most public discussion of terrorism has focused on moral conflict. Here both terrorists and counter-terrorists have a lot to say, often describing the situation very starkly as one of Good versus Evil. A rhetorical good-versus-evil position is used both by victims and perpetrators. It has a short-term political payoff. The speaker gets credit for taking a strong moral position while the listeners can invest the abstract categories with whatever content they choose to bring. The stratagem soon wears thin, however, because it does nothing to extend moral understanding. It simply plugs into existing prejudices and stifles a searching discussion of causes and implications of terrorism.

Moral arguments about terrorism draw on at least three different core ideas: moral community, human rights and the consequences of actions. The different positions are easier to grasp and to evaluate if you know what principles are being invoked. To add to confusion, some of the debate is about what grounding is the right one and commentators sometimes shift ground depending on whose actions are being judged, theirs or the enemy's.[1]

Moral community Both the choice to commit terrorism and the feeling of outrage against it stem from a sense of membership in a moral community whose members protect each other. Such a sense of membership is often nourished by stories about the founding of the community, stories in which terrorism and counter-terrorism may figure prominently. The story of the founding of the US includes both the Indian Wars of the colonial period and the War of Independence. In either conflict terrorism was an adjunct to warfare. Gangs murdered families and burned settlements. Israel finds its beginnings in the suffering of the massive terrorism of the Holocaust and in a few militant terrorist actions. Massacres in several Palestinian villages spurred the flight of the established population. A truck bomb at the King David Hotel in Jerusalem killed dozens of British citizens and pressured the British to withdraw troops and to leave the Israeli fighters to secure control of the territory for their new state. India and Pakistan were born in a disruptive division of the British colony that included huge killings of Hindus in Pakistan and Muslims in India. Although the agony and disruption of the movement of 14 million people to the 'right' side of the new borders turned out to be much more deadly than the acts of terrorism.

If Palestine becomes a state, terrorism will have been part of its foundation. Other nationalist movements – Irish, Basque, Corsican, Tamil, Kurdish, Serbian and others – also have (or had) terrorist offshoots that believe violence against civilians is justified under the circumstances – a way their moral community can gain expression as a state. In Algeria, Angola, Kenya and elsewhere terrorism contributed to winning political independence. Franz Fanon, the insightful critic of colonialism and false decolonization, thought in 1959 that attacks against settlers could help unite a population splintered and demoralized by the pervasive violence of colonial oppression. Fanon believed a violent struggle – at first desperate and uncoordinated – would gradually create a common identity among

peasants, intellectuals, workers and urban unem-
ployed. Together they would begin to construct a
healthy political community.[2]

Fanon had a point: and now more than 40 years later
terrorism has joined the experience of war as a shared
bleeding and bloodletting that can define a national
community. The legacy of terrorism for productive politics, however, remains questionable. Fanon clearly
underestimates the destructive effect of terrorism.
Nations, like Algeria, born in a cycle of reciprocal violence have proved no better at establishing workable
practices of peaceful political conflict than were those
which achieved independence through negotiation.
Arguably they are worse.

The most common rationale for state terrorism is
defense of the moral community that is the nation. In
killing Jews, Romas and homosexuals the Nazis asserted they were defending the Aryan nation against racial
and moral pollution. Ethnic cleansing in Cambodia,
Rwanda, Bosnia and elsewhere has been justified along
similar lines. Stalin claimed both Mother Russia and
the international working class as communities whose
opponents and betrayers ought to be eliminated.

A sense of moral community also colors the *response*
to acts of terrorism. The metaphor of war in defense of
a 'good community' is often used to justify extraordinary and arbitrary state powers. US commentators
express outrage at the way terrorists abuse democratic
freedoms to launch their deadly attacks and portray
them as especially vile enemies of civic morality who
have lost all claim to the ordinary rights of community
members. The US Government has drawn practical
conclusions from this moral position. Under the US
Patriot Act federal authorities can effectively detain res-
ident noncitizens indefinitely without charging them
with any crime. The underlying rationale is that they
are not part of the community of Americans protected
by the Constitution. Even citizens believed by federal
authorities to have worked with al-Qaeda or another

enemy can be labeled 'enemy combatants' and imprisoned until hostilities cease. In effect they lose the rights
conferred by community membership. By government
fiat they are stripped of constitutional protection.

Leaders who believe their state is engaged in a war
against terrorists may push their counter-terrorist
actions to the point of killing civilians linked to the
enemy. Some argue that Israel's attacks against
Palestinians have crossed the line that divides legitimate counter-terrorism from state terrorism. The
commitment of many Israelis to defend their state is
deepened by their belief that Israel was founded to
end the vulnerability of Jews that made the European
Holocaust possible. Some supporters of Israel's protective purpose reason that it justifies extraordinary
measures of defense.

Palestinians make a parallel argument about their
right as a people to a protective state in their ancestral
homeland. They see their struggle as a response to the
theft of their land to create Israel, in effect the cancel-
lation of their right to form their own national state.
Families cling to the papers that record their right to
land and the keys to houses long destroyed. The desire
of the Palestinians living on the West Bank to escape
the humiliation and hardship of Israeli occupation
adds to the will to struggle. Given the overwhelming
superiority of the Israeli army and various security
services, many Palestinians reason that all Israelis are
their enemies and targeting civilians is fully justified.

Many active political movements today claim that
religious belief is the proper basis for a morally-
grounded political community. Every religion has the
potential of inspiring followers to back their beliefs
with political authority. Religions assert grand truths
about good and evil and the rules that ought to govern
human interactions. The more urgently the claims are
felt and the more dangerous the battalions of evil
appear to be – the more attractive is the appeal to give
their faith a political form. This may include taking

armed and deadly action to rout the enemies and preserve the faith. Adherents of political religions that differ profoundly over religious doctrine all agree that the secular political ideal is morally bankrupt. Their descriptions of the materialist, world-dominating enemy can be startlingly similar. Terrorist groups inspired by their versions of Christianity and Islam denounce look-alike conspiracies of Jews, communists, capitalists and freemasons led by the US Government and the United Nations.

In situations of conflict, commitment to moral community is often the main justification for going to war. Such is the justification of the declaration by George W Bush of the right of the US to strike first at rogue states, terrorist states and terrorists. He believes that striking against enemies of the US moral community is always defensive and always justified. Once a government or a group sees itself as engaged in a war to defend the community it represents, it is a small step to employ weapons that will kill many civilians, torture prisoners to gain essential intelligence or send a suicide bomber on a mission. The *'jihad'* proclaimed by Osama bin Laden takes such a step – with his call for attacks on US citizens, as well as officials and military personnel. Such proclamations are often merely symbolic rather than practical, but they are still designed to reinforce a sense of moral community among potential followers.

Moral commitment to a group, of course, has real virtues. It can smooth collaboration among community members and make authority legitimate. It may even give grounds for recognizing that other communities have valid claims. To be consistent nationalists have to admit other nations may also have a moral right to a homeland. Reciprocity is one of the bases for a possible resolution to conflicts. Palestinians and Israelis for example could reciprocally recognize a 'two-state' solution. Both sides have a moral claim to a state complete with a sovereign government and territory in

Israel/Palestine. The issue then is where to draw boundaries and how to assure mutual security. However, the attachment of the claims of moral community to particular areas of land complicates the matter. Some Israelis living in West Bank settlements regard their right to this land is absolute and God-given. Palestinians must exercise their national rights elsewhere.

Some Palestinian organizations, like Hamas, believe all Israeli claims to land in the region are invalid. Israelis must exercise their national rights elsewhere, not on the stolen land they now occupy. The identification of territory with moral community stands in the way of negotiated solutions in many conflicts marked by terrorism around the world.

From the Hamas charter

The Islamic Resistance Movement believes that the land of Palestine is an Islamic Waqf consecrated for future Muslim generations until Judgement Day. It, or any part of it, should not be squandered: it, or any part of it, should not be given up.

Nationalism, from the point of view of the Islamic Resistance Movement, is part of the religious creed. Nothing in nationalism is more significant or deeper than in the case when an enemy should tread Muslim land. Resisting and quelling the enemy become the individual duty of every Muslim, male or female. A woman can go out to fight the enemy without her husband's permission, and so does the slave: without his master's permission.

In face of the Jews' usurpation of Palestine, it is compulsory that the banner of Jihad be raised. To do this requires the diffusion of Islamic consciousness among the masses, both on the regional, Arab and Islamic levels.

It is necessary that scientists, educators and teachers, information and media people, as well as the educated masses, especially the youth and sheikhs of the Islamic movements, should take part in the operation of awakening (the masses).

Mutual social responsibility means extending assistance, financial or moral, to all those who are in need and joining in the execution of some of the work. Members of the Islamic Resistance Movement should consider the interests of the masses as their own personal interests. They must spare no effort in achieving and preserving them. They must prevent any foul play with the future of the upcoming generations and

People who take their political values from Christianity and Islam, religions that claim universal validity, may assert that their rules of morality are valid for all people no matter what they believe. Some fervent believers think that in forcing nonbelievers to comply with the true morality, they are doing God's work. Colonial autocrats forced their subjects to work without pay and expropriated their best land in the name of a Christian civilizing mission – the right of a more evolved community over a more primitive one. The many-layered term 'jihad' in Islamic thinking is best translated as 'struggle'. It can refer to a personal spiritual struggle to accept the full truth of Islam. For some Muslims it can also refer to a defense of Islam by violence if necessary against the aggression of nonbelievers and believers in

anything that could cause loss to society. For a long time, the enemies have been planning, skillfully and with precision, for the achievement of what they have attained. They strived to amass great and substantive material wealth which they devoted to the realisation of their dream. With their money, they took control of the world media, news agencies, the press, publishing houses, broadcasting stations, and others. They were behind the French Revolution, the Communist revolution and most of the revolutions we heard and hear about, here and there. With their money they formed secret societies, such as Freemasons, Rotary Clubs, the Lions and others in different parts of the world for the purpose of sabotaging societies and achieving Zionist interests. With their money they were able to control imperialistic countries and instigate them to colonize many countries in order to enable them to exploit their resources and spread corruption there.

They were behind World War I, when they were able to destroy the Islamic Caliphate... They were behind World War II, through which they made huge financial gains by trading in armaments, and paved the way for the establishment of their state. It was they who instigated the replacement of the League of Nations with the United Nations and the Security Council to enable them to rule the world through them.

The Zionist plan is limitless. After Palestine, the Zionists aspire to expand from the Nile to the Euphrates. When they will have digested the region they overtook, they will aspire to further expansion, and so on. Their plan is embodied in the 'Protocols of the Elders of Zion', and their present conduct is the best proof of what we are saying. ∎

www.mideastweb.org/hamas.

false forms of Islam. During the crusades and inquisitions Christians, too, have defended a conception of their religious community with arms and resorted to terrorism. To the many people standing outside these circles of religious 'truth', the claims to universal validity seem false and intrusive. The values they assert belong to large, but still limited, moral communities.

Christian Identity politics

The place is Elohim City, an isolated religious community in the Ozark Mountains of eastern Oklahoma. Led by a bearded former Canadian Mennonite preacher named Robert Millar, it is home to seventy-five men, women, and children who are true believers in the religious doctrine known as Christian Identity.

By reinterpreting the biblical story of creation, practitioners of Christian Identity believe they have discovered a cosmic justification for modern-day racism. According to this reinterpretation, the origins of the Asian and African races lie in biblical 'beasts of the fields' – beings of an order lower than humans, whose existence predates God's creation of Adam 'in his own image'. Adam was not the first man, but the first white man. As the Christian Identity version of the Creation story unfolds, the serpent, disguised as a white man, gets into the Garden of Eden and seduces Eve, who bears the devil – a son in the form of Cain. That's how the Jews get into the picture. Demonizing Jews has a lengthy history in Western culture, but for contemporary racists, Christian Identity provides the ultimate proof that Jews are indeed the 'spawn of Satan'. Their evidence is even more convincing than the Protocols of the Elders of Zion, the faked 19th Century document which purported to be proof of a worldwide Jewish conspiracy. Identity followers draw their anti-Semitism and racism from the Bible.

Although the connections are seldom made by the media, Christian Identity provides the ideological backbone of such groups as the Aryan Nation, which seeks to claim the western mountains as a white homeland; the Midwestern Posse Comitatus, a militant underground which believes that the local sheriff is the highest legitimate elected official in the land; and Freemen groups like the one that held law enforcement authorities at bay in Montana in 1996.

On a more practical level, Christian Identity enclaves provide a trail of safe havens for movement activists, stretching from Hayden Lake in northern Idaho to Elohim City on the Oklahoma/Arkansas border. ■

James Ridgeway, Institute for First Amendment Studies, July/August 1997.

This notion of moral community tends to confirm a nonnegotiable starting point and to justify extreme measures: If we = good, then any enemy = evil. Any conflict moves into a stark bipolarism pushing for the exclusion of outsiders and often into warfare. There can be no compromise with evil. If you are not with us, you are against us. There is no difference between leaders and followers, soldiers and civilians, instigators and (possibly reluctant or ignorant) supporters. In such a simplified and distorted world, terrorism against those who stand outside the 'true moral community' is absurdly easy to justify. Immoral actions thus are warranted as means for defending morality itself.

Universal rights A larger moral framework recognizes that many different and competing claims to a moral community exist. It attaches political authority not to any particular religious or cultural vision, but to the right of anyone to have and to pursue such visions. Moral understanding need not stop at the boundary of one community; it grounds itself in universal values.

A set of influential intellectuals in the United States issued a statement about the evil of the September 11 terrorists and the justice of prosecuting a war against them that put the argument in terms of universal moral principles. The US had to defend such universals as civic freedom, freedom of religion, and protection of the human person. War is morally necessary when it is required to defend innocent people whose rights are under attack and who are in no position to defend themselves. A war so justified must be fought by a legitimate authority employing violence proportionate to the danger. The statement made clear that not all the cultural values, social tendencies and government policies in the US are worthy of support. But it argued that the core US values are valid and universal. A war fought to defend these values against terrorists is a just war. Such a war must never target non-combatants, although unintended killing of innocents may be unavoidable.

In the abstract the argument appears strong: a secular state committed to human rights may have to defend the right to have such rights. In practice the argument comes down to a political judgement. As the editor of the *Wall Street Journal*, Robert Hartley, put it in the 17 June 2002 edition, the supporters are saying that the US, whatever its faults, is 'a force for good in the world'. The signers agree, it seems, with President Bush's words on 1 June 2002 to cadets at West Point: 'America has no empire to extend or utopia to build. We wish for others only what we wish for ourselves – safety from violence, the rewards of liberty, and the hope for a better life.'

Bush might, however, have lost the support of some of the signers when he announced in the same speech that his government reserved the right to strike first at any government or group that the US believes is about to launch an attack on the US or its allies. Here we see how crucial is the question of who defines and enforces universal human rights. The US has been most reluctant to recognize the authority of any international body to do so.

Yet the very universal rights championed by the US are also the starting point for some of the critics of the war on terrorism, many of them US citizens. These critics accept the same constitutional and moral precepts that support democratic governance and civil and human rights but arrive at different political judgements. They believe that on balance the US is not a force for good in the world. Critics like Noam Chomsky readily marshal the evidence – the overthrow of elected governments in Iran, Guatemala, Indonesia and Chile; the training and financing of the Contra terrorists in Nicaragua; the support for President Suharto of Indonesia in his genocidal take-over of East Timor; the material assistance to President Saddam Hussein in Iraq when he was suppressing Kurdish nationalists with poison gas; and the cooperation with Pakistan and Saudi Arabia in training and arming the Taliban to destabilize the government of Afghanistan. Chomsky believes the world's most powerful government uses violence quite routinely and quite effectively to defend its economic interests. In doing so it stands against the 'hope for a better life' of most of the world's people. This position concludes that the most important step that the US can take to decrease terrorism is to stop engaging in it.

The invective in the altercations between these two 'universal rights' positions is especially acrimonious. They agree on the moral premise that humans universally have a right to freedom, security and democracy. They even agree that the record of the US

Jihad

The word Jihad means striving. In its primary sense it is an inner thing, within self, to rid it from debased actions or inclinations, and exercise constancy and perseverance in achieving a higher moral standard. Since Islam is not confined to the boundaries of the individual but extends to the welfare of society and humanity in general, an individual cannot keep improving himself/herself in isolation from what happens in their community or in the world at large, hence the Qur'anic injunction to the Islamic nation to take as a duty 'to enjoin good and forbid evil'. It is a duty which is not exclusive to Muslims but applies to the human race who are, according to the Qur'an, God's viceregent on earth. Muslims, however, cannot shirk it even if others do. The means to fulfil it are varied, and in our modern world encompass all legal, diplomatic, arbitrative, economic, and political instruments. But Islam does not exclude the use of force to curb evil, if there is no other workable alternative. A forerunner of the collective security principle and collective intervention to stop aggression, at least in theory, as manifested in the United Nations Charter, is the Qur'anic reference '...make peace between them (the two fighting groups), but if one of the two persists in aggression against the other, fight the aggressors until they revert to God's commandment'.

Military action is therefore a subgroup of the Jihad and not its totality. That was what prophet Muhammad emphasized to his companions when returning from a military campaign, he told them: 'This day we have returned from the minor jihad (war) to the major jihad (self-control and betterment).' ■

About Islam and Muslims from www.unn.ac.uk/societies/islamic/index

in supporting these rights is not pure. They further agree that the people who brought down the World Trade Center and damaged the Pentagon are a real menace and must be stopped. The two groups disagree about whether the US Government should be the sole arbiter of who is and who is not a threat to universal human rights. The critics of the US want to

---

US intellectuals justify war

What we're fighting for

To seek to apply objective moral reasoning to war is to defend the possibility of civil society and a world community based on justice.

The principles of just war teach us that wars of aggression and aggrandizement are never acceptable. Wars may not legitimately be fought for national glory, to avenge past wrongs, for territorial gain, or for any other non-defensive purpose.

The primary moral justification for war is to protect the innocent from certain harm... If one has compelling evidence that innocent people who are in no position to protect themselves will be grievously harmed unless coercive force is used to stop an aggressor, then the moral principle of love of neighbor calls us to the use of force...

The danger to innocent life is real and certain, and especially if the aggressor is motivated by implacable hostility – if the end he seeks is not your willingness to negotiate or comply, but rather your destruction – then a resort to proportionate force is morally justified.

A just war can only be fought by a legitimate authority with responsibility for public order. Violence that is freelance, opportunistic, or individualistic is never morally acceptable.

A just war can only be waged against persons who are combatants... Thus, killing civilians for revenge, or even as a means of deterring aggression from people who sympathize with them, is morally wrong. Although in some circumstances, and within strict limits, it can be morally justifiable to undertake military actions that may result in the unintended but foreseeable death or injury of some non-combatants, it is not morally acceptable to make the killing of non-combatants the operational objective of a military action...

These principles strive to preserve and reflect, even in the tragic activity of war, the fundamental moral truth that 'others' – those who are strangers to us, those who differ from us in race or language, those whose religions we may believe to be untrue – have the same right to life that we do, and the same human dignity and human rights that we do. ■

Signed by many US academics and intellectuals
12 February 2002 http://www.americanvalues.org/

strengthen international courts and bodies to make such judgements and enforce them. The supporters of the US record on balance trust the US to make the correct determination over the long run.

Consequentialism Many who think about the moral meaning of terrorism are less interested in the abstract rightness or wrongness of particular terrorist acts or counter-terrorist measures than in what they accomplish and for what interests. They judge actions in terms of their consequences. Consider the case of terrorist acts by a committed group in the name of a worthy goal such as overthrowing a rapacious dictator. Or consider state terrorist measures employed to defeat a monstrous and clever political sect. Might not the end be worth the means? Would not a few deaths and a time of fear among certain people result in a much safer and freer outcome for the majority? Is that not a good moral bargain?

Obviously we cannot know the future, so consequentialist moral reasoning works better in hindsight than in prospect. The sociologist Barrington Moore argues that the death and suffering of the French Revolution, including the Terror, had the beneficent consequence of destroying social institutions of inequality and exploitation that were day after day grinding millions of lives into pain, despair and death. He judged this a good bargain from a long-term historical point of view.[3] Yet such judgements are hard to make, even historically. Judging events and actions before their consequences are known is much trickier still. The value of a judgement based on highly uncertain predictions is obviously compromised. Yet political leaders have to make such judgements all the time.

Political leaders are powerfully drawn to consequentialist moral reasoning on many policy issues. Damming a river harms some people and even destroys ways of life, but it helps others. The politicians in charge evaluate the balance of benefits and costs – no

doubt giving special weight to influential powerhold-
ers and to the impact on their own careers. The same
kind of reasoning can be applied to the distribution of
violence. War planners try to deliver damage and
death to enemy forces in the most efficient and effective pattern. They can and do also consider the
benefits and costs of doing violence to civilians.
Bombing Dresden will cause fire storms and kill tens
of thousands of civilians. But perhaps it will demoral-
ize the German high command, shorten the war and
save the lives of allies and Germans alike. A suicide
bomb in Tel Aviv will kill dozens of ordinary Israelis
and trigger an Israeli attack on a West Bank refugee
settlement that will kill Palestinians. But it will also
recruit more suicide bombers and strengthen the radical Palestinian faction against the moderates and
further the cause of restoring what is now Israel to the
Palestinians. This is the way reasoning about the consequences of killing civilians justifies terrorist actions.

Consequentialist reasoning is used effectively against
terrorism as well. Even in the case of terror or state terror that seems to promote benefits such as enhancing
the power of a democratic state or weakening an evil
government, opponents can argue that the consequences will be the creation of more enemies and the
use of valuable resources needed elsewhere. This argument has been used by the Palestinian critics of suicide
bombing and by opponents of the war on terrorism.

The consequentialist version of the terrorism
debate often turns on the moral importance placed on
enhancing state power. Machiavelli argues that the
end of enhancing state power justifies the means of
state violence against enemies and opponents who
might otherwise weaken the state. For him state power
is more than an end in itself; it alone makes civic order
and social morality practically possible. Those who
support the power of a given state often follow
Machiavelli's reasoning. They back the use of state terror as a regrettable necessity for achieving the benefits

the state brings over the long run. Those who oppose the extension of state power are often less critical of the terror of groups that attack the state because the damage people suffer looks small compared to the suffering the state inflicts.

Three big ideas

Debates about terrorism are colored by historical ideas as well as by moral standpoints. The ideas used to explain terrorism often turn out to be connected to a vision of one of the big themes in our current history. There are three major themes here. Some familiarity with them helps in finding a way through the commentaries and debates that swirl around the war on terrorism. Each is in its own way too general and too weakly linked to any actual terrorist act to provide a full explanation of terrorism. At best each can give a partial insight into the context out of which terrorism emerges, But these ideas have another kind of importance – despite their weaknesses they guide the thought of planners of terrorist acts and of shapers of counter-terrorism policies.

Failed modernization The most frequently-encountered big idea is failed modernization. The core idea here is that some societies have been unable to achieve the promise of growth in material wealth in a secular, science-based and democratic society. Two variants of the theme give it quite different interpretations. The neo-conservative variant argues that the opportunity to modernize is there for any society to seize. Countries like Taiwan, South Korea and Singapore provide examples of transformation into productive, relatively high-income market societies in a couple of generations. Failures are the responsibility of rulers and populations who did not take advantage of the opportunity to emulate the West by leapfrogging to the latest technologies. Persistent corruption, the wrong ideology, ancient conflicts or other misadventures have kept

societies off the globalization train. Some fall into the
abyss of failed or collapsed states unable to discharge

Noam Chomsky: terror and just response

Those who do not rise to the minimal moral level of applying to themselves the standards they apply to others – more stringent ones, in fact – plainly cannot be taken seriously when they speak of appropriateness of response; or of right and wrong, good and evil.

Consider a case that is far from the most extreme but is uncontroversial; at least, among those with some respect for international law and treaty obligations. No one would have supported Nicaraguan bombings in Washington when the US rejected the order of the World Court to terminate its 'unlawful use of force' and pay substantial reparations, choosing instead to escalate the international terrorist crimes and to extend them, officially, to attacks on undefended civilian targets, also vetoing a Security Council resolution calling on all states to observe international law and voting alone at the General Assembly (with one or two client states) against similar resolutions. The US dismissed the [Court] on the grounds that other nations do not agree with us, so we must 'reserve to ourselves the power to determine whether the Court has jurisdiction over us in a particular case' and what lies 'essentially within the domestic jurisdiction of the United States' – in this case, terrorist attacks against Nicaragua...

There could hardly be a clearer example of international terrorism as defined officially, or in scholarship...

Consider some of the legal arguments that have been presented to justify the US-UK bombing of Afghanistan; I am not concerned here with their soundness, but their implications, if the principle of uniform standards is maintained. [International Law professor] Christopher Greenwood argues that the US has the right of 'self-defense' against 'those who caused or threatened... death and destruction,' appealing to the [World Court] ruling in the Nicaragua case. The paragraph he cites applies far more clearly to the US war against Nicaragua than to the Taliban or al-Qaeda, so if it is taken to justify intensive US bombardment and ground attack in Afghanistan, then Nicaragua should have been entitled to carry out much more severe attacks against the US...

The same holds of more nuanced proposals about an appropriate response to terrorist atrocities. Military historian Michael Howard proposes 'a police operation conducted under the auspices of the United Nations... against a criminal conspiracy whose members should be hunted down and brought before an international court, where they would receive a fair trial and, if found guilty, be awarded an appropriate sentence.' Reasonable enough, though the idea that the proposal should be applied universally is unthinkable... ∎

ZNet 2 July 2002, www.zmag.org

even minimal government functions. The poverty and political instability that ensue breed frustration, calls for change, violence and even terrorism. They create conditions of urban anarchy and rural warlordism in which terrorists can gather, hide and prepare.

These neo-conservatives believe that even the richest of the developed economies and the most powerful political and military establishments cannot reverse or resolve all the failures of modernization. The best response is an agenda of self-protection – keeping the dangerous places under close scrutiny and going after terrorists when they appear. The governments of all countries, including those where terrorists gather, have a duty to crack down hard on these dangerous people.

The left-wing variant of failed modernization locates the weakness in the modernization model itself which benefits rich countries at the expense of the poor. It simply does not fit the real possibilities of many countries, including large parts of Africa and the Middle East. The worst of the inequality, instability and poverty that breed and hide terrorists is remediable. The rich and powerful should reform the model of modernization and invest the money and effort needed to bring substantial benefits to the countries and regions most in need. This step will reduce the anger and frustration that breed terrorism, but action may still be necessary to deal with existing terrorist organizations.

Failed modernization, unfortunately for its proponents, itself fails to find the particular causes behind many episodes of terrorism. What about terrorism in paragons of modernization like Japan (*Aum Shinrikyo*) and Germany (Red Army Faction)? Why has Sri Lanka in recent years suffered from separatist terrorism and not Malaysia? Why are the crisis-ridden economies of the Caribbean less troubled by terrorism (state and group) than those of Central America? Modernization is in serious trouble, no question. But as a theory of terrorism it is too broad and vague. It stands in the way of understanding.

Clash of civilizations A second way of seeing the big
picture from which terrorism arises is the Clash of
Civilizations, a phrase made famous from the titles of
an article (1993) and a book (1996) by Samuel
Huntington. The collapse of communism, according
to this perspective, shifted the major lines of conflict
in the world to the cultural. Supporters of this perspective find verification in Europe's Middle Ages
when Muslim rule expanded into Spain and attempted to push into France, or when Christian crusades
attempted to wrest control of Jerusalem from its
Muslim rulers. But their main interest is the future:
'The dangerous clashes of the future are likely to arise
from the interaction of Western arrogance, Islamic
intolerance, and Sinic [Chinese] assertiveness', says
Huntington. The theory is elaborated from a frankly
pro-Western perspective and designed to shape policy.
The implication is that Westerners should expect
recurring conflict with Islamic and Asian political powers. No amount of modernization will make 'them'
more like 'us' and our observance of values we regard
as universal will not end the major differences.[4]

Unfortunately, accepting the clash of civilizations as
an organizing idea obscures insight into the actual
variety of bases of terrorism. Cultural differences are
without doubt an important source of conflict; but, so
too are competition for resources like petroleum,
water and land. Moreover, citizens, whatever their culture, are still stirred to vigorous opposition by
experience with self-serving and corrupt concentrations of power that torture citizens and deny them
basic rights. Differences of identity within the global
cultures Huntington names, especially those stirred by
nationalist claims, remain potent. The growing dispar-
ity of incomes within and between countries keeps
ideologies of right and left alive in social movement.
Among recent terrorist episodes, many have nothing
to do with a clash of civilizations: the leftist claims of
the red groups in Europe; nationalist claims within a

cultural zone of Basques in Spain, Kurds in Turkey and Tamils in Sri Lanka; the obscure rural revolutionary goals of *Sendero Luminoso* in Peru; and the defense of the unborn by anti-abortion militants in the US. Cultural differences feed into political conflict, but to see terrorism through the lens of a clash of civilizations is a dangerous and blinding simplification.

Primary and secondary terrorism A third perspective, put forward most coherently by Edward Herman and Gerry O'Sullivan in *The 'Terrorism' Industry* focuses on state terrorism and downplays the importance and danger of group terrorism.[5] It locates the problem of terrorism in a large historical dynamic: the 'primary terrorism' of Western colonial expansion and continued economic and political domination provokes a 'secondary terrorism' of desperate response to the suffering and injustice inflicted by this primary terrorism. This analysis does not excuse or condone secondary terrorism, but it places historical responsibility for terrorist problems squarely in the hands of the Western perpetrators of primary terrorism. The historical causal force stimulating terrorist activity is Western expansionism and Western efforts to retain worldwide economic and political dominance. This perspective credits the claims often put forward by popular movements in the global South that the political settlements ending colonial rule were unjust and that post-colonial government is often the tool of Western economic and political interests. Its core equation is that the elimination of the injustices and relations of domination perpetrated by Western industrial powers will remove the *raison d'être* of terrorism.

This perspective captures one of the great waves of modern history that is too often neglected by writers looking at terrorism: the fundamental and often extreme violence of Western colonial expansion and the continuing resort to violence to retain post-colonial domination. It tends to ground itself on a few cases where evidence of US involvement in terrorism is strong, such as the mining of Nicaragua's harbor in support of Contra terrorism. But it makes no survey of a cross-section of terrorist acts and groups since the Second World War to see how well they fit the theory. It ignores the terrorism inside Europe from ETA in Spain to the Red Army Faction in Germany, but is markedly Euro- and US-centric when it comes to weighing the causes of terrorism in Latin America, Asia and Africa. It sees state terrorism in Brazil, Chile and Argentina and the Indonesian army slaughter in East Timor as the responsibility of the US. Is there no responsibility of those governments for their own actions?

Where the US failed to oppose state terrorism – even where it supported a security apparatus that engaged in such terrorism with money and training – there remains room for some moral and political autonomy on the part of 'client' governments. Governments that are in no way simple clients, like Myanmar (Burma) or Zimbabwe, are quite able to engage in state terrorism. Most former colonies and dependencies inherited an autocratic government and severe economic and political difficulties from their colonial experience, but terrorist regimes are prominent in only a few places. Nor can group terrorism automatically be traced to colonial violence and injustice. The idea of primary and secondary terrorism falls short as a general explanation of terrorism. Holding it too tightly stands in the way of understanding the many cases it fails to illuminate.

A less comprehensive theory of Western action and terrorist response is much more convincing with respect to specific cases and gives insight into the origins of state terrorism, a topic carefully ignored by many terrorism experts. It takes the name 'blowback', as noted in chapter three, from the term used inside the CIA for the unintended consequences of initial interventions. The US gave Saddam Hussein's regime in Iraq support to make it a stronger counterweight to

Iran, but then President Hussein turned that power both against Iraq's Kurdish population and toward the invasion of Kuwait. The US gave assistance to the Taliban via Pakistan's intelligence agency (and perhaps more directly) in order to strengthen a promising opponent of the Soviet occupation of Afghanistan. The Taliban succeeded admirably and turned its success to support of al-Qaeda and other Islamist terrorist organizations. In these cases the 'blowback' resulted in an increase of terrorism turned against US interests.[6]

Oddities of the moral-historical debate

Each of the three above perspectives paints the troubling terrorist episodes of the present on a much larger historical canvas. They appeal to existing prejudices and invite us to fit our understanding of today's terrorism into a familiar and comfortable formula. Their main function is to bolster a worldview that supports a broad policy stance with a combination of historical and moral-political interpretation. In their general forms they are of limited help in the task of understanding terrorism.

The neo-conservative idea of failed modernization suggests that Western policy can do nothing much of use for 'basket-case' countries. George Bush reflected that attitude during the election campaign in 2000. He replied to a question about assistance to Africa: 'I don't think nation-building missions are worthwhile.'[7] When basket-cases are also incubators of terrorism requiring some kind of response, the main actions that are likely are military ones or counter-terrorism that tends to mimic the terrorism it opposes. Here again a wide-ranging historical theory limits policy ideas.

A deeper and more troubling issue is raised by the core idea of failed modernization: might modernization itself, even the seemingly successful type, sometimes breed discontents that can transmute into terrorism? Many of the terrorists in the West and Japan are children of relative privilege offended by the inequalities and injustices they connect with modernization. They seem to resent the lack of meaning and moral purpose in the culture of industrial capitalism. Their search for a cause beyond the normal politics of market society can set them on a path that leads to terrorism. It might be that the bland power of self-satisfied market élites will always be provocative for the searching idealism of the young, drawing a few into a political calling that promises to be more exciting and morally-grounded than any their society has on offer?

Some critics have argued that policy and rhetoric built on the idea of a clash of civilizations will tend to produce such a clash: the theory becomes self-fulfilling. The angry reaction in the Muslim world when President Bush called for a 'crusade' against terrorism confirms the danger of the symbolism of the Christian West versus Islam. The US leader never repeated that phrase and went out of his way to deny that Islam was in any sense the target or the enemy. Yet the phrase lingers on as an explanation for the pattern of US actions in the Middle East and in the war on terrorism.

Moralistic thinking can also narrow policy options and moralistic talk can undermine diplomatic efforts. People react where they see a whole nation or religion being called evil. They are also alienated when one government asserts a monopoly on the ability to define, perceive and defend universal human rights. A useful quality of consequentialist moral reasoning is that it forces the thinker to go beyond moral labeling to consider the social dynamics and end results of a particular action. The obligation to consider actual consequences can be very troubling to someone who wants simply to assert a categorical moral law or defend a moral community.

In the immediate aftermath of a terrorist attack, those harmed and aggrieved react as people wronged. They want their sense of violation to be shared, acknowledged and supported. Seeking to understand the grievances, motives and contexts out of which the attack might have grown is of no immediate interest to them. Even to raise such questions is offensive to many. After the attacks of 11 September Americans who questioned the effectiveness of the US response were dismissed as America-haters and near traitors – even if they condemned the attacks as monstrous crimes. Those not immediately involved can more easily turn their attention to the causes and contexts of frightful attacks. After 11 September European commentators did this, much to the annoyance of many Americans.

The different forms of reasoning produced strange altercations over mentioning 'root causes' of terrorist attacks. For one-dimensional defenders of the US or Western moral community, even to think in this way was like finding excuses for the devil's penchant for evil.

The US leaders who in the 'war against terrorism' assert the categorical 'evil' of those they label terrorist adopt consequentialist reasoning about the actions of their own side. Thus defenders of the US bombing of Afghanistan acknowledge that many innocent civilians have been killed, but then point to the positive results of the military campaign: girls are now in school, children are vaccinated and food aid is getting through to hungry people. Moreover, they claim that they made

The ordinary American

Anti-Americanism is one of those prejudices that musters evidence to suit a conclusion already in place. For it, ordinary Americans can never be just that. They can certainly never just be victims, a status already monopolized elsewhere. Americans, or 'the West', are blithely dehumanized into the molecules of a structure, what bin Laden calls America's 'vital organs'. As for their government, its policies amount to a condition, an essence. The actions of various mass murderers (the Khmer Rouge, bin Laden) must, rightly, be 'contextualized.' But to the anti-American, American policy never has 'context.' It is. ■

Todd Gitlin, 'The ordinariness of American feelings', 10 October 2001, http://www.opendemocracy.net

extensive efforts to minimize civilian casualties. On balance, they argue, more citizens of Afghanistan are living and living freer and better than they would have been without the bombing.

Debate about such claims can be clarifying. Critics of the morality of bombing argue that civilian deaths are much more numerous than US officials admit and that unexploded bomblets and mines remain deadly dangers. They further claim that the new government is unstable and leaves known terrorist warlords in power to continue their terrorist ways. The gain in freedom for women is, they believe, overstated. They point to a dramatic increase in general lawlessness and insecurity. The harvest of poppies and the export of heroin have resumed, once again to finance terrorist groups in Central Asia and beyond. Such a debate covers matters that need to be investigated and taken into account in evaluating the military strategy in Afghanistan and in considering possible future action. But the argument is seldom joined in this manner. Each party tends to excuse its own violence against civilians using consequentialist reasoning while condemning the violence against its own civilians in terms of universal human rights or violation of a moral community.

From the perspective of making good policy choices that will minimize negative consequences, the case for examining contexts and causes is pragmatic and powerful. If terrorism is produced by a social process that can be analyzed, then to rid the world of terrorism or even just to reduce its incidence, it makes sense to address these causes and contexts. Some leaders and commentators will get behind the emotional reflex to kill or punish the aggressors, but those who search a more considered response will *think* as well as feel. They will carefully weigh up the consequences of all possible retaliatory actions before they act.

The days that followed 11 September in the US are a telling example. The search for causes and consequences was scorned, at least publicly. An instant orthodoxy sprang to the lips of most leaders and commentators: al-Qaeda, Osama bin Laden and the Taliban had chosen the path of evil and had to be wiped out. The Afghan factions who fought alongside the Americans and who followed their established practice of 'bargaining' with the enemies were portrayed as moral cripples. But a more consequentialist approach would raise questions about why the enemy engages in terrorism and how they might be induced to abandon that path. It obliges the analyst to pursue kinds of understanding that do not start with simple moral invocation. It would raise questions of history, organization, leadership and social dynamics. Such questions lead to a kind of thinking that goes beyond just condemning terrorism to treating it as a social phenomenon that needs to be understood. This is the domain of military thinkers, policy analysts and social scientists who claim membership in the small group – the 'terrorism specialists'. From their offices and institutes they have gathered, weighed and analyzed a mass of information. And, as the next chapter will show, they have developed some interesting ideas.

1 RG Frey and Christopher W Morris, *Violence, Terrorism, and Justice*, edited by RG Frey, Cambridge Studies in Philosophy and Public Policy. (Cambridge: Cambridge University Press, 1991). **2** Frantz Fanon, *The Wretched of the Earth*, (New York: Grove Press, 1963). **3** Barrington Moore, Jr., *Social Origins of Dictatorship and Democracy: Lord and Peasant in the Making of the Modern World* (Boston: Beacon Press, 1966). **4** For citation sources see Robert Kaplan, 'Looking the World in the Eye,' *Atlantic Monthly*, December 2001. **5** Edward Herman and Gerry O'Sullivan, *The 'Terrorism' Industry: The Experts and Institutions That Shape Our View of Terror* (New York: Pantheon Books, 1989). The most useful part of the book is the detailed catalogue of state terrorism and the connections with US government agencies as well as the identity, funding and orientation of the long list of research institutes that specialize in terrorism. **6** Chalmers Johnson, *Blowback: The Costs and Consequences of American Empire* (New York: Henry Holt, 2000). **7** Presidential Debate at Wake Forest University 11 October 2000.

5 Between war and politics

The war on terrorism discounts the political side of terrorism and displaces politics with warfare. Governments discourage popular political action and shrink the range of political debate. A better response would vigorously combat terrorism as a crime. But it would also cultivate democratic action on the vital material and cultural issues that are crying out for creative political attention.

MOST OF THE world has noticed the existence of a fundamental global economic asymmetry between North and South going back decades. But with the demise of the Soviet Union and the degradation of Russia's military capacity, planners in the US see a new kind of asymmetry. No country can challenge militarily the supremacy of the single superpower. Well-connected analysts are looking hard at the implications of asymmetry for US defense posture. They are calling into question almost every part of the defense establishment: training, tanks and other equipment, division into services, size and type of operational units and communications systems. Most importantly they are proposing a new doctrine to govern the changed art of war and arguing about how to fight it. They call it 'asymmetric warfare' or 'fourth generation warfare'.

The new doctrine calls attention to a new kind of enemy, one that is detached from state structures and devoid of conventional military weapons and tactics. The enemy is terrorism. All big industrial powers have military machines that are overwhelmingly more powerful than any terrorist group. Terrorism cannot threaten their military superiority. The danger of terrorism for the big powers is economic and political disruption. The complex integration of advanced economies and communications makes them vulnerable to attacks on such key elements as energy supplies, financial networks, information systems, population concentrations and symbols of national pride. Disruption is not military defeat, but it jolts the economy, tarnishes the reputation of the government of the day and interferes with its ability to extend its economic and cultural influence around the world. The governments of big powers are making major efforts to do something about the risks of terrorism. The question is: what can they do? Experts in asymmetric warfare think they have the answer in a new military posture, but a close look at their reasoning suggests an alternative response.

Their analysis looks beyond the military balance to the social and political map of the world. It draws on the idea of failed modernization discussed in chapter four. It goes something like this: in a world marked by extreme economic inequality and rapid social change, cultural friction ignites movements with extreme religious and political claims that sometimes turn to terrorism. The movements challenge and sometimes destroy the integrity and stability of weaker states.

Some movements pursue strictly local goals such as more autonomy for their region. Even those, like the Tamil Tigers, with nationalist goals may confine their action to their country or region. Others give their local struggles a transnational reach, as Black September did when it killed eleven members of the Israeli Olympic team in Munich in 1972 in an operation designed to free comrades and further the Palestinian cause. International groups, notably al-Qaeda, may draw energy from local conflicts, but they operate internationally and pursue transnational goals. Al-Qaeda's mission is the kind the North's military planners worry about most. It wants to forge a new political unity for Islam, reshape political control of the oil-rich Middle East and weaken the power and ambition of the industrial North, particularly the US.

The social asymmetry that worries the military planners is concentrated in sprawling cities of the South

like Karachi and Jakarta, lawless zones like northeast-
ern Pakistan and the Triple Frontier where the borders
of Argentina, Brazil and Paraguay meet and whole
countries such as Lebanon and Somalia marked by
endemic conflict involving externally-funded terrorist
groups. Such places are crowded with young, diverse,
underemployed populations with minimal government
control. Here movements capable of terrorism find a
supportive environment to recruit and train followers.
A clandestine trade in weapons, drugs and cash opens
the way for terrorists to act both locally and globally.

From a military standpoint, the planners note, the
very strengths of the great industrial democracies can
be used to the advantage of terrorists operating globally. Terrorists can abuse the freedom of information,
movement, communication, education and acquisition in Western democracies to orchestrate terrorist
attacks. Mohamed Atta, reputed to have headed the
terrorist team that led the 11 September assault took
full advantage of the freedom to meet and the means
of communication and travel he found in Hamburg
to plan the attacks. American society was wide open to
anyone wanting to learn basic flying skills. For military planners civil rights are a handicap in the war on
terrorism.

The experts also believe that the technical and political organization of the US and other wealthy
market-oriented democracies that makes them powerful also makes them vulnerable. The highly integrated
systems of information, communication, finance and
energy flow on which advanced societies depend are
impossible to protect from determined attack. The
WTC held a concentration of financial information
and handled a huge flow of communication and
transactions. The attackers may well have intended to
damage the system.

Technical innovations add to the scope for terrorist
action. Cell phones and the internet make transnational coordination easier. Computer programs for

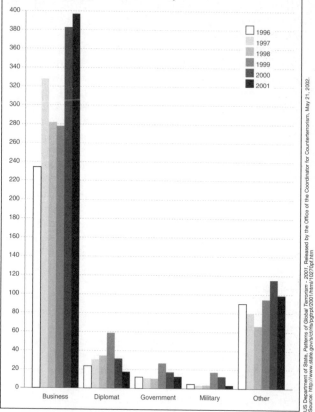

Civilian targets bear the brunt of terrorist attacks

The distribution of attacks from year to year among kinds of targets is much more stable than their distribution among countries. Compare with graphic on page 29, 'Moveable mayhem'.

Legend: 1996, 1997, 1998, 1999, 2000, 2001

Categories: Business, Diplomat, Government, Military, Other

US Department of State, Patterns of Global Terrorism - 2001. Released by the Office of the Coordinator for Counterterrorism, May 21, 2002. Source: http://www.state.gov/s/ct/rls/pgtrpt/2001/html/10270pf.htm

acquiring, storing, communicating, encrypting and organizing all kinds of information can be purchased. Flight simulating programs turn a notebook computer into a device for learning to fly. Newer kinds of explosives are more powerful for their weight and more easily handled and detonated. Terrorists learn from experience and search out new kinds of vulner-ability in the societies they want to attack. The counter-terrorist thinkers say that terrorist actions have become more destructive in the last few years. There were a rising number of deaths per incident even before September 2001, although the number of incidents was declining.

The theorists emphasize that the greatest danger is that group terrorists will get their hands on the weapons that buttress the military superiority of the strong states: nuclear, biological and chemical (NBC) weapons capable of harming whole cities or regions. Al-Qaeda's leaders, reports say, were trying to acquire chemical and biological weapons and had an interest in nuclear weapons. They considered crashing a bomb-filled airplane into a nuclear reactor. In Japan, *Aum Shinrikyo* did release Sarin nerve gas in the Tokyo subway. By good fortune their method was faulty and the gas did not disperse properly, but six people were still killed. Ready access to international travel, com-munication and technical information and the spread of engineering skills – all aspects of globalization – make it impossible to confine the capacity to use NBC weapons to the big powers.

Asymmetric warfare theorists believe that terrorist tactics count on a classic principle of martial arts – turning the power of the society they attack to their own advantage. Transforming airplanes into missiles or fertilizer into bombs are just two examples of terrorists redirecting technology from production to destruc-tion. Typically, the weapons they favor (assault rifles and special explosives) were developed by the very gov-ernments they want to attack. Successful terrorism must redirect the social energy of the targeted society by provoking widespread public panic or by stimulat-ing an overreaction by governments that offends people and ends up strengthening the terrorist cause.

Looking into the future, the military analysts see the

expansion of economically-polarized, culturally-splintered and politically-ungoverned zones throughout the global South. Terrorist groups will become increasingly autonomous from any state sponsor. They will combine sophisticated transnational organization with locally-autonomous cells. Their weapons will gain in destructive power and be directed more frequently against strategic targets. They will also make increasingly effective use of mass media to spread fear, panic and confusion.

The military thinkers paint a daunting picture. A general sense of public gloom and panic is deepened by such issues as the HIV-AIDS pandemic in Africa and Asia, unchecked population growth in many regions, growing economic inequality within and between countries, more frequent floods and droughts, emergence of more disorderly megacities, a burgeoning black economy of drugs and contraband, expanding global corporations willing to do business with anyone if the price is right, sharpening conflicts over water and energy resources and repeated economic crises. Even the best intelligence with flexible and specially-trained forces and mobile equipment cannot realistically hope to stop such a gathering storm. The forecast by the leading hawks in the US administration, US Defense Secretary Donald Rumsfeld and Vice-President Dick Cheney, calling for never-ending war seems well founded.

A different reading

Fortunately there is another way of reading the analysis of asymmetric warfare. Military specialists tend to take the asymmetric evolution of the globe as an unalterable given – a fact of nature. Their job is to devise a military solution to the problem it poses. However, the asymmetric conditions they emphasize are neither inevitable nor facts of nature; they are the outcome of policies and actions driven by the very countries most exercised by the terrorist danger. The theory of asymmetric warfare sees a collapse of distinctions between battlefield and homeland, soldier and civilian, combat and politics. The conventional conclusion is to broaden the notion of enemy and develop ways of attacking and killing small groups, even individuals, anywhere in the world. The US is perfecting and implementing new technologies of information-gathering and imaging. The drone reported to have killed a wanted al-Qaeda member and four companions in Yemen in November 2002 exemplifies the new military doctrine in action. Military targets must be broadened and military capabilities made more flexible. The society at home must accept new forms of surveillance and be kept on constant alert. Military thinking must colonize more and more of political space.

A few analysts look at the same picture and draw a very different conclusion:

> If these or similar [political and economic] factors are indeed driving the evolution of conflict, then solutions must lie primarily in this arena, that is within the realms of economics, diplomacy, and law-enforcement. Military force will play a smaller role, performing specific tasks to solve problems that are intractable through other means. A coherent 'grand strategy' is needed to ensure that military (destructive) actions harmonize with our overall objectives and do not provoke a backlash that negates tactical success. Technology is not unimportant, and may provide options, but the fact is that lack of suitable technology cannot explain our less-than-stellar track record in fourth generation warfare.[1]

There are two assertions here with profound implications. The first is that a prevalent kind of terrorism cannot be defeated militarily. It has no state sponsors and therefore is less vulnerable to military strikes. Moreover, since it espouses causes that are gaining legitimacy in the eyes of many, military strikes will provoke a dangerous political backlash. Therefore, the war on terrorism can hardly be 'fought' in a military sense and certainly cannot be 'won'. The second assertion is that the conditions that give rise to terrorism and make it such a difficult enemy can be altered through diplomatic, economic and political action. Here is room and reason to tilt away from seeing terrorism as mainly a military problem to seeing it as a social/economic/political one. On a global scale it means addressing some of the great issues of modernization gone wrong.

A third theme can be added to this alternative reading of the theory of asymmetric warfare. The usual analysis exaggerates the danger posed by terrorism to the big industrial countries. The quick recovery from the destruction of such an important hub of financial transactions and information exchange as the World Trade Center shows that the system is less vulnerable than feared. The economy of Sri Lanka survived when the LTTE bombed the country's central bank and financial center. Pipelines, oil tankers and fuel depots have been targeted by terrorists in Colombia, the Persian Gulf and Israel without much impact on energy supply. The lumping together of nuclear, biological and chemical weapons in the term 'weapons of mass destruction' disguises the very different dangers these weapons represent. Nuclear weapons are by far the most destructive and by far the least likely to be used by terrorists. Scenarios of terrible attacks using chemical weapons can be imagined, but dispersal is quite difficult and its scope is likely to be limited. Biological weapons are potentially self-propagating, but their use may be discouraged by the fact that they also endanger the people they are meant to help or to avenge. Appallingly destructive attacks are possible, but disasters like Bhopal (4,000 dead, hundreds of thousands injured in a chemical leak in 1984) and the HIV-AIDS pandemic (in Botswana 36 per cent of sexually active adults test positive) show that even poor societies cope with chemical and biological disasters.

The symbolism and the psychological impact of targets and weapons still seems more telling than their economic effect. Bigger airplanes, office buildings and stadiums offer terrorists larger and symbolically more attractive targets. Chemical and biological agents and 'dirty bombs' could bring nightmares to waking life and have enormous political consequences. This *mise-en-scène* has not escaped the notice of producers of disaster movies who trade on a similar symbolism to that of the terrorist: in the gruesome world of high explosives and mass poisoning does art imitate life or is it the other way around?

All terrorism is local

A closer look at terrorism in operation confirms the importance of its political side. All terrorism is rooted in local contexts. Even the movements with global reach like al-Qaeda and Hizbullah began in a distinct region and gave voice to particular grievances. It is true that terrorists like Abu Nidal or Carlos the Jackal became guns-for-hire willing to operate almost any-where. But they get hired by movements or governments acting in a particular context. Most ter-rorist organizations emerge not in failed states or chaotic zones of bloated megacities but in countries with relatively stable governments: Ireland, Egypt, Spain, Algeria, Colombia, Sri Lanka, Italy and the US. These are not failed states, although some have become less stable under the impact of terrorism. The role of failed states and unstable zones – Lebanon, Palestine and Afghanistan fit the model rather well – is less as generators of terrorism than as places of refuge where terrorists may gather, train and organize.

To understand terrorist organization we need to grasp how it connects with the local context. Knowing the social background of terrorist activists provides important clues. Take two examples:

• In the year that President Nasser hanged Sayyid Qutb, the writer and activist who advocated replacing Egypt's Arab socialism with an Islamist state, a 15-year-old boy from a family of prominent Cairo doctors and educators founded a cell in his high school devoted to keeping Qutb's ideas alive and working to overthrow Nasser's government. The year was 1966 and the boy was Ayman al-Zawahiri, later to merge the Egyptian Islamic Jihad with Osama bin Laden's al-Qaeda organization and to become the chief strategist and organizational manager of al-Qaeda. The Egyptian dissident sociologist, Saad Eddin Ibrahim, who has studied Islamist activists in his country explains that typically they are 'model Egyptians' from educated middle class families. The parents are often government bureaucrats or professionals. Al-Zawahiri once bragged to a visiting American that most of members of his Islamist group were from the élite university faculties of medicine and engineering.[2]

• Abimael Guzmán Reymoso, founder and leader of *Sendero Luminoso* in Peru until his arrest in 1992, was also a middle class university student drawn to revolutionary action in the mid-1960s as a result of directly observing the plight of the underclass. In Guzmán's case the inspiring ideology was communism and the underclass was the poor and landless peasantry of Ayacucho, where Guzmán taught philosophy. He explained to his captors in 1992, 'Their reality shook my eyes and my mind'. Already as a student he had found compelling the writings of Jose Carlos Mariategui, a founder of Peruvian socialist thought, and Stalin, whom he called 'a great Marxist-Leninist, a great man' despite his 'mistakes'. Guzmán initiated a guerrilla and terrorist conflict in 1980 that lasted a dozen years and killed an estimated 30,000 Peruvians in a brutal cycle of terrorism and counter-terrorism. Most of those who died were poor peasants in whose name Guzmán launched his struggle.[3]

If the leaders of terrorist organizations are usually from the middle class, many of the rank and file members come from poorer and rougher backgrounds in the refugee camps, shanty towns and neglected countryside. The social service side that is a vital part of some terrorist organizations has a presence in places where unemployment is more common than employment. Along with social services they provide an explanation of the surrounding misery and the promise of a disciplined approach to doing something about it.

The large nationalist movements recruit widely from the popular classes. The parties to violence in Ireland like the Catholic Provisional IRA and the Protestant Ulster Volunteer Force draw from the

Women and terrorism

• Even the phrase 'women terrorists' heightens the sense of extremism and irrationality that is attached to terrorism. In the 1950s people were shocked when women members of the Algerian FLN planted bombs in cafes and cinemas during the campaign against French rule. The idea of women or girls as suicide bombers is especially disturbing to many people. What are their motives? How are they indoctrinated? Such questions are rarely asked about men, as if terrorism and suicide missions are normal outlets for young male urges. Women are more frequently seen as mothers or wives, often gravely supporting the terrorist cause. Their most familiar role is that of victim, whether as casualties in indiscriminate attacks in public places or special targets for rape and physical abuse. Calls for action against terrorism often invoke the deaths of 'innocent women and children' as reason for harsh reprisals.

Yet women as leaders and warriors in terrorist groups are not unusual. Leila Khaled received international publicity and became a role model for her cool elegance in hijacking a TWA flight from Rome to Athens in 1969. The mission, her first for the Popular Front for the Liberation of Palestine, ended with all hostages released unharmed. Two armed women were among the four Palestinians who hijacked a Lufthansa flight from Majorca to Frankfurt in 1977. They demanded money and the freeing of Red Army Faction prisoners in Germany. One of the women was killed and the other wounded when a German anti-terrorist squad stormed the plane in Mogadishu.

Among the leaders of the Red Army Faction were two women, Ulrike Meinhof and Gudrun Ensslin. Women were well-represented among active members and leaders in the left-wing terrorist organizations of Europe and North America. Many of them came to terrorism from university activism and many had family ties with other members of organizations that engaged in terrorism. ■

The Sociology and Psychology of Terrorism: Who Becomes a Terrorist and Why? US Library of Congress, Washington DC, September 1999 working class. FARC in Colombia, LTTE in Sri Lanka and PKK in Turkey attract activists from low-income rural and urban backgrounds.

The European and Japanese left-wing and anarchist terrorist groups of the 1970s, on the other hand, drew their members mainly from the middle class. Most of them had some university education; many began their activist career while in university. For example the Red Army Faction (also called the Baader-Meinhof

Terrorist movements sometimes make a point of recruiting women. The Tamil Tigers have recruited many women as suicide bombers. In Palestine the secular al-Aqsa Martyrs' Brigade has sent more women on suicide missions into Israel than the more religious groups.

Robin Morgan, as an active member of the Weather Underground in the US, opposed the male dominance she encountered inside the group. From her own experience and a study of terrorism she concludes that 'the central knot of terrorism' is 'the intersection of violence, eroticism, and what is considered ìmasculinity.' To succeed, any action against terrorism must dethrone the idea of the violent, single-minded, controlling and self-sacrificing hero/martyr. Women, too, she says come under the enchantment of this idea and some willingly serve as helpers, supporters and lovers of terrorists. She and others believe that women have the compassion and vision to work against terrorism and the violence that is bound up with patriarchy. The Women's Peace Movement in Northern Ireland, Women in Black in Israel and Palestine, and mothers' clubs in Peru, for example, all work to end the violence of conflicts that include terrorism. ■

Robin Morgan, *The Demon Lover: The Roots of Terrorism*, New York: Washington Square Press: 2001, p. xvi.

• American officials have found that assigning a female interrogator to a case can throw some [imprisoned al-Qaeda] suspects off stride. ■

Eric Schmitt, 'There Are Ways to Make Them Talk', New York Times, 16 June 2002

• Zoria Shrfaei, head of the Algerian association for defending women's rights, stated that the number of women who were raped by terrorist groups reached 5,000, citing statistics that 1,313 women were raped between 1994 and 1997 and that more than 2,000 were kidnapped and killed in year 1997. In 1998 the government opened the first center to take care of women raped by terrorists. ■

26 February 2000 and 19 October 1998: http://www.arabicnews.com

Gang) included among its members Gudrun Ensslin, daughter of an evangelical church pastor, Suzanne Albrecht, daughter of a wealthy lawyer; Andreas Baader, son of a historian; Ulrike Meinhof, daughter of an art historian; Horst Mahler, son of a dentist; and Holger Meins, son of a business executive.[4]

These cases confirm that the material grievances of the poorest and most exploited are not often the mainspring of terrorist action (although in anti-colonial violence and peasant uprisings landless peasants sometimes attacked settlers who had occupied their land). In itself poverty rarely imparts the emotional energy that is evident in acts of terrorism. The springs of terrorism lie rather in a sense of humiliation, degradation and disrespect. Poverty and exploitation are important as marks of the humiliation visited upon the people with whom one identifies. The commentators who assert that material suffering has nothing to do with terrorism because so many terrorists are middle-class simply fail to see that the connection between poor living conditions and political action passes through a feeling that the group with which one identifies is held in contempt.

Not blind rage

Terrorism is not striking out in blind rage. It is considered action that takes account, however perversely, of a social and political context. Even the impoverished and exploited farmers and workers who engage in nationalist terrorism are fighting for self-rule and self-respect for the group with which they identify. Their action is inspired by social and symbolic goals and grievances. Poverty and exploitation for them are important as marks of humiliation and degradation rather than as primary motives. For middle-class terrorists the significance of ideas and ideologies is even more striking. The kind of personal experience that feeds the anger or hatred that some of them carry is often physical or social humiliation inflicted upon a family member, a close associate or oneself. One of the mechanisms that keeps the cycle of terrorism and counter-terrorism going is the reciprocal and deliberate effort to humiliate the other side. Thus by intention and by circumstance does the cycle of terrorism/counter-terrorism perpetuate itself.

Grievances and anger never lead directly to terrorist action. People, usually young people, have to be recruited to terrorism and their loyalty and obedience maintained. Local contexts and the immediate incentives are crucial here. Big forces of social dislocation have to feed into an effective local strategy for a terrorist organization to thrive. Enduring terrorist organizations become part of the local social landscape. They are one of the 'career choices' which local youth may adopt. Where employment is hard to find and career paths rare, terrorist activism may seem a viable choice. The terrorist entrepreneur with a knack for recruiting young men and women, much like the enthusiastic organizer of a youth club, often has a key role to play.

Many commentators remark on the charismatic appeal of Osama bin Laden and credit it for al-Qaeda's influence among dissatisfied Arab and Muslim youth. Local conflicts and the personal magnetism of recruiters combine with the particular adolescent angst of a young person or a group of young friends to produce success for terrorist entrepreneurs. An impressive terrorist attack and a repressive counter-terrorist response can trigger successful recruitment. The attack symbolizes the potency of the organization and its cause; the repression confirms the view that terror tactics are morally legitimate and practically necessary. According to leaders of Islamic Jihad, al-Qassam Brigades and Hamas there is no shortage of volunteers for suicide missions following an Israeli assault in the occupied territories. Hatred of the occupation is often compounded by the death or injury of friends by Israeli military action. Resistance actions are commemorated in 'revenge songs'.

A terrorist organization must also have a way of organizing and educating that confirms and retains the interest and commitment of new recruits. Terrorist organizations use several, often contradictory, methods for retaining loyalty. On the positive side are rituals that inspire feelings of camaraderie and belonging to a larger cause. The videotapes made by suicide bombers on the eve of their sacrificial violence express adherence to both cause and family. They convey the serenity of total commitment. Leaders, present and past, become heroes to emulate. Material support for recruits and their families lends recognition and may compensate in some part for the loss to a family of a lifetime of earnings. The governments of Iran and Iraq, and wealthy Saudis are all reported to contribute to funds that make payments to the families of suicide 'martyrs'.

On the negative side, recruits can be kidnapped and pushed into actions that make them criminals wanted by the authorities. Fear keeps such recruits in line. The main purpose of a cell structure is to prevent the capture of any one member from unraveling more than a single cell in the larger organization. But it also can play a role in controlling lower-level recruits. The lack of horizontal communication among cells prevents recruits from talking to one another and sharing any grievances they may have. Threats and intimidation may neutralize any move against the local leadership.

Where an identity group is fighting for political autonomy and where terrorism has become part of an ongoing way of life as in Northern Ireland, Palestinian refugee camps and Tamil towns and villages in northern Sri Lanka, terrorist organizations, like youth gangs in many western cities, are a powerful magnet for boys and girls approaching adulthood. Peer pressure, family tradition and exemplary heroes play a part in the choice made. Youth who do not abhor violence and who want to be true to the beliefs of their fathers and mothers will be drawn in. Their leaders know how to identify the best prospects and guide them into terrorist activity.

In the case of organizations defined by a political ideology like the Red Army Faction, the Red Brigades and the Weather Underground the path to terrorism is often quite different. Young people in the European or North American context may also be searching for meaning in their lives, but end up at odds with the social and political stance of the adult world including their parents. There are many accounts of better-off young people who, in a period of soul-searching about their future, come under the influence of a radical spokesperson or group that plots a convincingly different course for them. Typically the new course struggles against apparent and real injustices from which their inherited life plan would profit. Those who rebel have a sense that they are acting on principles that their parents hold only rhetorically. Young militants in a national struggle – as in Israel, Palestine, Northern Ireland, Basque country and Tamil country – work to revive a homeland that earlier generations were unable to defend. Or they may feel they are choosing commitments quite opposite to their parents' hated ideals, as was the case of some members of the Red Brigades in post-fascist Italy and the Red Army Faction in post-Nazi Germany.

Inner workings

The workings of state terrorist organization are not that dissimilar to non-state ones, although states have much larger budgets and accepted processes for recruiting and paying soldiers. State-run proxy organizations in comparison to non-state groups are likely to give more importance to material incentives and less to ideology. Some government leaders may slide into state terrorism without thinking much about it. They are already using violence in instrumental and symbolic ways: imprisoning and perhaps executing criminals, incarcerating security risks and bombing enemies.

Their power of life or death, freedom or prison may be exhilarating even if legal. It is not a big jump to start acting outside the law in the name of *raison d'État*.

Beliefs about identity and ideology can move government leaders just as they do group terrorist leaders. Their moral compass may justify attacks against both internal opponents and external enemies. Doctrines of national security, Nazism and communism can be shaped to persuade the rank and file of the need for terror tactics. One of the most common justifications for perpetrators of state terrorism is that they act in the name of counter-terrorism to defend the dignity and power of the state. Beneath the rhetoric, simply hanging onto power is often a major motive. The revered leader is often invoked as the 'great explainer' who assumes responsibility for the 'necessary' politics of terror.

The art of shaping cadres of young people, usually men, into willing torturers and killers is well honed and well known to military establishments. The key is to unite a sense of larger mission (defending the nation) with a sense of group loyalty and interdependence (fighting for one's comrades). Armies have long been adept at such training, isolating the trainees from family and society and using boot-camp techniques to reinforce obedience to the chain of command and loyalty to a team of soldiers. The military and civilian managers of military operations are imbued with a belief in the strategic value of aggression and violence in the pursuit of certain national or regime interests. The very same combination of strategic aggression and group dependence has often been turned to purposes of state terrorism. The commander of a special unit need only declare that certain people are enemies of state security and the soldiers' license-to-kill can be directed against that group. Philip Zimbardo's famous psychology experiment at Stanford University in 1971 that placed students in the roles of prisoners and guards in a simulated prison showed how rapidly ordinary young men could be turned toward torture. The experiments had to be ended abruptly after only six days because the 'guards' subjected the 'prisoners' to sadistic treatment.[5]

The larger mission that cements state-terrorist resolve may be a nationalist ideology, but it may also be a sectional loyalty within a culturally segmented country. Many national leaders in poorly integrated countries are best seen as warlords with a sectional base who have seized national power. They may cement support in one region or one group while focusing repression on a region or a group represented as alien or disloyal. A skillful and ruthless leader like Saddam Hussein can direct a security service recruited from a favored group to undertake terrorist action against a vilified minority. Saddam Hussein's poison gas attack on the Kurdish population of Halabja in 1988 was also a warning to opponents in other regions of the punishment that might await them.[6]

Living dangerously

Many participants in terrorist organizations become attached to the excitement of danger, secrecy and dissimulation. There is the rush of living outside the rules, getting away with doing what is forbidden. In the case of suicide bombers the cult of martyrdom and an acceptance of death in the name of a great cause are sufficient. State terrorists may gain the sense of being part of the specially-formed 'professional' team authorized to use criminal violence for patriotic reasons.

Potential recruits and their families also may be making a rational calculus about how their security and well-being are most likely to be enhanced and least likely to be damaged. Their local worlds are penetrated by many kinds of division and conflict. It is not unusual for families to place sons in more than one local faction in order to hedge their bets and to preserve some useful contact with all parties. The complexity of the family ties and personal networks is sometimes surprising.

Families knit connections on both sides of divisions that appear superficially to be unbridgeable.

Globalizing terrorism and counter-terrorism

The military strategists of asymmetric warfare may overemphasize the globalization of terrorism, but they signal a real trend that US policy has inadvertently encouraged. Al-Qaeda was greatly strengthened when al-Zawahiri merged Egyptian Islamic Jihad with Osama bin Laden's group. Its recruits from dozens of countries shared the experience, supported by the US, of training and fighting in Afghanistan and forged a new kind of transnational identity for the organization. Intelligence experts believe it also had training centers in the Philippines and Indonesia. Its core was flexible enough to make use of the strengths of its branch operations. It remained active and effective even after the US-led invasion drove al-Qaeda from its base in Afghanistan. Expert observers believe it emerged from the ordeal more decentralized and more dangerous than ever.[7]

Intelligence sources familiar with information about al-Qaeda often compare it to a transnational corporation with active branches in many countries, some of them independent franchises. Moreover, just as McDonald's inspired Burger King, al-Qaeda's example, they believe, is prompting the formation of look-alike organizations. Local cells and regional centers are loosely linked through interpersonal and ideological networks. The network is reinforced by meetings and training camps and by channels for collecting and transferring funds.

The US as the leader of the war on terrorism tries to globalize counter-terrorism by drawing governments into a common policy of military and police action against terrorists of all stripes. Governments are pressed to enact tough security legislation and to crack down on groups suspected of international connections. Often, as in the case of Indonesia, they are offered military assistance and military training.

Sometimes, as in the Philippines, the US supports cooperative governments with troops as well as economic assistance.

The war on terrorism gives al-Qaeda, and terrorism in general, a strong global image. States facing any kind of insurgency claim they are fighting the global terrorist enemy. Russia puts Chechen separatists in this category, in order to garner international support and legitimacy, especially from the US. Some Chechen insurgents find it useful to adopt the garb of radical Islam and deliver videotaped messages to al-Jazeera television. Like other local movements they are drawn to represent themselves as part of a global endeavor in order to gain publicity and international support for their cause.

Facing a common enemy, diverse locally-based movements work to enhance their collaboration. Experts believe Hizbullah with a Lebanese base, Iranian backing and a radical Shi'a ideology is now collaborating with al-Qaeda with its radical Sunni Islam. Terrorist organizations as different as Colombia's FARC, the IRA and Hamas appear to have collaborated on matters of training and equipment. They now have a common interest in learning how best to operate in a climate shaped by the War on Terrorism.

What the war on terrorism does

For governments the war on terrorism fills a void that appeared with the end of the Cold War and the spread of neo-conservative views that governments should shrink and scale back their programs. It gives governments something important to do and supplies a ready reason to strengthen instruments of internal security and to monitor or restrict potentially troublesome political movements.

The fight against communism or imperialism was reason enough in Cold War days for governments to expand their power. With the demise of state communism the US reduced support for repressive anti-communist regimes. Democracy movements and competitive politics spread widely in the unipolar world. Democratic movements are often disrespectful of sitting governments and they can generate conflict that brings political order itself into question. Many governments discovered reasons to fear democracy. The war on terrorism gives them the opportunity to play on the widely-felt sense of vulnerably to reinforce their power. Governments the world over are beefing

Legislation on terrorism – India

In response to heightened national security concerns, and as relations with Pakistan deteriorate and violence in Kashmir and elsewhere escalates, the Indian Government introduced the Prevention of Terrorism Ordinance (POTO), a modified version of the now-lapsed Terrorists and Disruptive Activities (Prevention) Act (TADA) of 1985, which facilitated the torture and arbitrary detention of minority groups and political opponents. POTO was signed into law by the President on October 24 2001 to remain in effect for six weeks. It was introduced as a bill during India's winter session of parliament and was passed on March 27.

Under TADA, tens of thousands of politically motivated detentions, torture, and other human rights violations were committed against Muslims, Sikhs, Dalits, trade union activists, and political opponents in the late 1980s and early 1990s. In the face of mounting opposition to the act, India's government acknowledged these abuses and consequently let TADA lapse in 1995. Civil rights groups, journalists, opposition parties, minority rights groups, and India's National Human Rights Commission unequivocally condemned POTO.

Now enacted, the Prevention of Terrorism Act (POTA) sets forth a broad definition of terrorism that includes acts of violence or disruption of essential services carried out with 'intent to threaten the unity and integrity of India or to strike terror in any part of the people.' Since it was first introduced, the Government has added some additional safeguards to protect due process rights but POTA's critics stress that the safeguards don't go far enough and that existing laws are sufficient to deal with the threat of terrorism. Shortly after POTA was approved by parliament, Richard Boucher, State Department spokesperson, declared that the bill was 'within constitutional bounds' and India had strengthened its legal system to combat terrorism in a manner 'consistent with democratic principles'. ■

Human Rights Watch,
http://www.hrw.org/campaigns/september11/opportunismwatch.htm

up police and intelligence agencies and implementing legislation that curtails political liberties and reduces protection against arbitrary arrest.

The war on terrorism draws attention away from issues of global inequality and degradation of living conditions that are important in their own right and remain important causes of conflict. Instead international bodies are swamped by issues of security. The global movement for economic reform finds its scope for action more limited. In the industrial North it finds governments are less open to discussion about economic justice. The public is encouraged to see the South more as a source of danger than a region in need of international economic and social reform. Activists have to commit energy and resources to defending human and civil rights and opposing the worst of the new security legislation. A coalition that might come together on many aspects of global economic reform and environmental defense is more divided when forced into dealing with issues of security and terrorism.

Debate about globalization is being choked off at a time when a new generation of activists is responding to the changing constellation of power and wealth in the world and participating in vital cultural changes and conflicts. Lively debates are under way on fundamental issues such as the political role of Islam, Christianity and Judaism; appropriate political structures for multicultural states and alternatives to orthodox market solutions to issues of stalled development and income maldistribution. These debates need wide publicity and broad participation. Liberal secularists need to debate why modernization is failing so many of the world's people. Instead they are caught up in arguing about the morality of putting huge amounts of money into weapons. Religious believers need to discuss how they can adapt their beliefs to a pluralism of faiths but instead are forced to defend their religion's basic morality. The politics of fear and power replaces a politics of intellectual challenge and practical give and take.

Legislation on terrorism after 9/11

Australia Antiterrorism legislation before Parliament includes proposals to proscribe certain groups and reduce rights for suspects in custody. Stricter asylum legislation was expedited after 9/11.

Canada The December antiterrorism act improved on earlier drafts, but risks of criminalizing peaceful activity and of unfair trials remain. Another new law hinders asylum applications. On April 29 the Government presented a bill on public safety under which the armed forces could declare 'controlled access zones' wherever military equipment is kept.

China After 9/11 Beijing intensified its crackdown on Uighur opponents of Chinese rule in Xinjiang, claiming they are linked to 'international terrorism'. Officials have reportedly detained thousands and placed new restrictions on the religious rights of Muslims. On December 29 China amended its criminal law to 'punish terrorist crimes, ensure national security and uphold social order'.

Colombia In February President Pastrana resumed the civil war in which all sides have committed atrocities. He announced that rebels would be treated as terrorists '[a]nd in that, the world supports us'. The Constitutional Court ruled as unconstitutional a national security law that would have strengthened impunity by giving police and judicial powers to armed forces in conflict zones. New security legislation is likely.

Germany New legislation expands grounds for rejecting asylum claims and enables banning groups that 'support organizations in or out of Germany that cause, threaten or practice assaults against persons or things or if they are a danger to public order and security.

Indonesia The Minister of Justice and Human Rights announced that a proposed antiterrorism bill to be submitted to the House of Representatives includes sentences that range from five years to death for disrupting security and damaging public facilities.

Jordan Amendments to the penal code in October expanded 'terrorism' to include damaging the environment; public, private, or international organizations; or diplomatic missions. They also strengthened powers to shut any publication producing 'false' or libelous information that could 'undermine national unity or the country's reputation'.

Pakistan The January Antiterrorism Amendment Ordinance will undermine judicial independence by bringing military officers onto panels of judges trying 'terrorist' offenses. These antiterrorist courts impose most of Pakistan's death sentences. Since 9/11 the Government has attempted to suppress demonstrations by religious parties.

Philippines Human rights groups report indiscriminate mass arrests and torture of suspected members of and sympathizers with the Abu Sayyaf Group, which allegedly has links to al-Qaeda. After an April 21 bombing killed 15 people, President Macapagal-Arroyo asked Congress to pass the pending antiterrorism bill. Currently, foreign 'terrorist' suspects are detained under old immigration law.

South Africa The draft antiterrorism bill could criminalize strikes and attempts by nonviolent demonstrators to deliver a petition to a foreign embassy. The bill also provides for detention without trial.

Spain A government-proposed law regulating political activism could ban political parties that encourage 'hatred, violence, and social confrontation'; challenge the legitimacy of democratic institutions; or 'promote a culture of civil confrontation'. The law is aimed at Batasuna, the political wing of the Basque separatist movement, ETA.

Uganda The March Antiterrorism Act introduces a mandatory death sentence for convicted terrorists. Publishing news 'likely to promote terrorism' can lead to a 10-year prison sentence.

UK The Antiterrorism, Crime and Security Act 2001 permits indefinite detention of non-UK nationals without charge or trial if the Home Secretary reasonably believes and suspects they are a national security risk and an 'international terrorist'. The belief and suspicion may be based on secret evidence.

US More than 1,000 people, most from Middle Eastern or Muslim countries, were arrested after 9/11; some 300 may remain in detention. The October US Patriot Act allows indefinite detention of non-deportable, non-US citizens if the attorney general has 'reasonable grounds to believe' they are engaged in terrorist activities or endanger national security. On November 15 President Bush issued a Military Order that non-US nationals accused of terrorism could be tried by military commissions, infringing rights to a fair trial.

Zimbabwe In the run-up to the March presidential elections, President Robert Mugabe labeled his opponents 'terrorists', thus appearing to condone violent attacks by his supporters on his political opponents. The Public Order Security Act allows police to ban demonstrations and criminalizes criticism of the police, army and president. A new Access to Information and Protection of Privacy Act allows the Government to ban newspapers and imprison journalists for articles that portray the Government in a negative light.

European Union A proposed comprehensive action plan envisages legislation on a European arrest warrant, an EU-wide definition of terrorism, an EU public prosecutions agency, an EU mechanism for freezing suspects' assets, examination of immigration and asylum laws, and a mechanism to prosecute computer crime. The definition of terrorism is broad enough to criminalize peaceful activities.

The Arab League In January Arab Ministers of the Interior agreed on measures to 'combat terrorism' and pledged to implement the Arab Convention for the Suppression of Terrorism. It defines 'terrorism' so broadly that it is open to abuse. It widens the scope of the death penalty in many countries. ∎

Amnesty International
http://www.amnestyusa.org/amnestynow/war_terrorism.html

The war on terrorism includes a well-funded and skill-fully-directed information component that raises the fear level and keeps attention on security. It sucks energy from other discussions and forces basic issues to the margins of public dialogue. The way the war on terrorism enables the US to shape the political agenda within the US, in international discussions and in many other countries may be its most impressive quality.

The worlds of industry and science are affected by the war on terrorism. They are turned significantly in the direction of creating technologies to defend against terrorism and to take effective action against

---

Legislation on terrorism – Egypt

In the immediate aftermath of September 11, Egyptian Prime Minister Atef Abeid lashed out at human rights groups for 'calling on us to give these terrorists their 'human rights', referring to documented reports of torture and unfair trials. 'After these horrible crimes committed in New York and Virginia, maybe Western countries should begin to think of Egypt's own fight and terror as their new model.' Egyptian security forces on September 20 arrested Farid Zahran and held him for fifteen days without charge, apparently fearing that a demonstration he was helping to organize to mark the first anniversary of the outbreak of Palestinian-Israeli clashes would raise criticism of the government's close ties with the US. The Government has also ordered nearly 300 suspected Islamists to be tried in three separate cases before the Supreme Military Court, despite their civilian status. According to defense lawyers, many had been imprisoned for years without trial. US Secretary of State Colin Powell subsequently noted that 'we have much to learn' from Egypt's anti-terrorist tactics, despite the fact that such tactics have been used against nonviolent critics as well and include emergency rule, detention without trial and trials before military courts. Egypt is 'really ahead of us on this issue,' Powell said. On December 16, President Mubarak asserted that new US policies 'prove that we were right from the beginning in using all means, including military tribunals…' In its most recent human rights report on Egypt, the State Department had said Egypt's military tribunals 'infringe on a defendant's right to a fair trial before an independent judiciary'. 'There is no doubt that the events of September 11 created a new concept of democracy that differs from the concept that Western states defended before these events, especially in regard to the freedom of the individual,' Mubarak said. ∎

Human Rights Watch,
http://www.hrw.org/campaigns/september11/opportunismwatch.htm

terrorists. The new knowledge and new weapons may strengthen counter-terrorism, but they will eventually almost certainly add to the weapons and techniques available to terrorists. Already the fruit of anthrax research designed to improve defense against bioterrorism has been turned against US politicians and media. Bystanders have died in these attacks. When the Russians used a new kind of incapacitating gas to subdue Chechen hostage-takers in Moscow it also demonstrated to terrorists a new way to attack civilians. All the talent and money invested in securing US military communications and in mining global communications to eavesdrop on terrorist planning are pulled away from other endeavors. They might have been used to find ways of conserving energy and water, one way to address a major source of conflict in the world.

The war on terrorism also draws attention away from arms control and arms elimination projects. Efforts to reduce the availability of land mines, light automatic weapons and explosives might have a direct effect on the frequency and deadliness of terrorist actions. Control of the production and distribution of nuclear, biological and chemical weapons (NBC) would lower the chances of terrorists making use of such weapons. These efforts are weakened and displaced by enlarged military budgets and accelerated production of weapons systems for possible counter-terrorist use.

The shift from politics to warfare in dealing with terrorism is not total. In several cases local terrorist movements have seen the new global rigidity in the face of terrorism and decided to abandon their more extreme claims and enter a process of political bargaining. The LTTE in Sri Lanka, the IRA in Ireland, FIS in Algeria, ETA in Spain and Kurdish groups in Turkey have all moved (some quite tentatively) in this direction. These are all movements with a strong popular base that will serve well in the transition to a more political form of struggle. The governments with which they negotiate may take a more flexible political position because they see the benefits of the support they receive as collaborators in this war. These cases demonstrate that a response to terrorism that responds to its political challenge is not a pipedream. It has practical potential.

A better response

If the major powers stopped regarding terrorism as primarily a military matter, they might begin working together to change the conditions that give rise to terrorism. A promising start would be joint efforts to reduce the number and size of the ungoverned and chaotic areas of the globe, improve the conditions of living in the world's megacities and diminish other sources of social crisis. Still dangerous terrorist organizations would continue to exist and make plans to strike. Several of them are well-established institutions with a drive to survive and effective modes of operating. The conditions out of which they grow and the conflicts they reflect will not soon disappear. Some outbreaks of terrorism are bound to occur even if global action diminishes their frequency.

Citizens are right to demand retaliation against terrorists. Governments are right to take action to assure the security of their citizens, with special effort to prevent the acquisition and use of NBC weapons by terrorist organizations or by states. Few dispute the necessity of a response, but the question of how to respond provokes controversy. There are strong reasons to reject the language and actions of a war on terrorism and to regard terrorist acts as crimes against humanity rather than acts of war. To do so avoids many of the negative anti-political effects of the war. It deprives terrorists of assuming the mantle of the heroic warrior and treats them instead as lowly criminals. Terrorism, whether committed by a state or group, is a crime in every country and is often on a scale that counts as a crime against humanity. The pursuit of terrorists as criminals requires action to uncover and abort terrorist

Responses to 'terrorism'

Governments around the globe are restricting human rights and political freedom in the name of fighting terrorism.

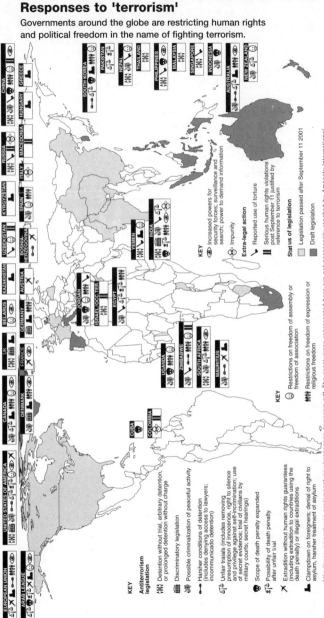

KEY

Antiterrorism legislation

Detention without trial, arbitrary detention, or prolonged detention without charge

Discriminatory legislation

Possible criminalization of peaceful activity

Harsher conditions of detention (includes denying access to lawyers; incommunicado detention)

Unfair trials (includes removing presumption of innocence; right to silence and privilege against self-incrimination; use of secret evidence; trial of civilians by military courts; secret hearings)

Scope of death penalty expanded

Possibility of death penalty after unfair trial

Extradition without human rights guarantees (including extradition to countries using the death penalty) or illegal extraditions

Clampdown on foreigners; denial of right to asylum, harsher treatment of asylum

KEY

Restrictions on freedom of assembly or freedom of association

Restrictions on freedom of expression or religious freedom

KEY

Increased powers for security forces; surveillance and search; power to demand information

Impunity

Extra-legal action

Reported use of torture

Serious human rights violations post September 11 2001 justified by reference to terrorism

Status of legislation

Legislation passed after September 11

Legislation passed after September 11 2001

Draft legislation

http://www.amnestyusa.org/amnestynow/responses_terrorism.pdf The conclusions represented here are not necessarily reached by Amnesty International operations. Police and special forces will have to do more than react to terrorist crimes once they are committed. Good intelligence is critical.

Diplomatic work to reduce conflict in all the regions that are caught in cycle of terrorism and counter-terrorist response could make a large impact in the total amount of terrorism committed. Some can be resolved and others can be diminished. When passion is removed from local violence and moved into political negotiation and confrontation the energy available to sustain terrorist efforts can be diverted. Work is also necessary on reducing state terrorism, decommissioning state-terrorist institutions and retraining former state terrorists. Unfortunately the war on terrorism provides a ready excuse to retain and expand organizations of state terrorism under the guise of counter-terrorist services.

The work in policing, intelligence and diplomacy that targets terrorism directly should not be allowed to draw attention from the other vital tasks. Work on adapting democracy, reforming the national and international economy, limiting and controlling weapons and organizing popular political action remain important for their own sake and are key ways to reduce the tensions and causes on which terrorism thrives.

The world will have to continue to live with terrorism. Governments and citizens can do a lot to limit its incidence. We badly need to curtail the damage it does to popular action and governmental work on the life and death political issues that face humankind.

1 Defense and National Interest DNI, Atlanta, Georgia, www.d-n-i.net. **2** Lawrence Wright, 'The man behind bin Laden', *The New Yorker*, 22 September 2002. **3** 'Exclusive' comments by Abimael Guzmán', *World Affairs* 156 no.1 (Summer 1993) p 52. **4** *The Sociology and Psychology of Terrorism: Who Becomes a Terrorist and Why?* (Library of Congress, September 1999). **5** www.prisonexp.org. **6** Jonathan Raban, *The Guardian*, 11 December 2002. **7** Susan Schmidt and Douglas Farah, 'Six Militants Emerge From Ranks to Fill Void', *Washington Post*, 29 October 2002, p A01.

CONTACTS

INTERNATIONAL

The Alternative Information Center
POB 31417, Jerusalem 91313, Israel
www.alternativenews.org/

Amnesty International
99-119 Rosebery Avenue
London EC1R 4RE, UK
www.amnesty.org/

CAIN Webservice
Conflict Archive on the internet
cain.ulst.ac.uk/cainbgn/index.html
Sources on the Northern Ireland conflict

**The International Policy Institute for
Counter Terrorism (ICT)**
www.ict.org.il/

**The International Rehabilitation
Council for Torture Victims**
Borgergade 13
PO Box 9049
DK-1022 Copenhagen
Denmark
www.irct.org/

Peace Brigades International
International Office
Unit 5, 89-93 Fonthill Rd
London N4 3HT, UK
Tel: +44-(0)20-7561-9141
Fax: +44-(0)20-7281-3181
Email: nfo@peacebrigades.org
www.peacebrigades.org/

Project Disappeared
http://www.desaparecidos.org/arg/eng.html
Piedras 153 1ªA, c.p.1070
Capital Federal
República Argentina
Tel/Fax: +54-11-4343-1926 5745
madres-lineafundadora.org/noticias/

The Terrorism Prevention Branch
UN Office for Drug Control and Crime
Prevention
Vienna International Centre
PO Box 500
A-1400 Vienna
Austria
www.undcp.org/odccp/terrorism.html

CANADA

Canadian Centre for Victims of Torture
194 Jarvis Street
2nd Floor
Toronto, Ontario
Canada M5B 2B7
www.icomm.ca/ccvt/

US

Center for Defense Information
1779 Massachusetts Avenue, NW, Suite
615
Washington, DC 20036-2109
www.cdi.org/

Federation of American Scientists
1717 K St, NW, Suite 209
Washington, DC 20036
www.fas.org/terrorism/index.html

Human Rights Watch
350 Fifth Avenue, 34th Floor
New York, NY 10118-3299
www.hrw.org/

The National Security Archive
The George Washington University
www.gwu.edu/~nsarchiv/

Southern Poverty Law Center
400 Washington Avenue
Montgomery, Alabama 36104
334/956-8200
www.splcenter.org/

US Department of State
Counter-terrorism Office
www.state.gov/s/ct/

Women in Black
www.womeninblack.net/

ZNet
18 Millfield Street, Woods Hole, MA 02543
www.zmag.org/ZNET.htm

BIBLIOGRAPHY

The CIA: A Forgotten History, William
Blum (London: Zed Books, 1986)
The Culture of Terrorism, Noam Chomsky
(Toronto: Between the Lines, 1988)
*Global Terrorism: the Complete
Reference Guide*, Harry Henderson
(New York: Checkmark Books, 2001)
Inside Terrorism, Bruce Hoffman (New
York: Columbia University Press, 1998)
*Terror and Taboo: The Follies, Fables,
and Faces of Terrorism*, Joseba
Zulaika and W. A. Douglas (New York:
Routledge, 1996)
Terror in the Mind of God, Mark
Juergensmeyer (Berkeley: University of
California Press, 2001)
*The 'Terrorism' Industry: The Experts and
Institutions That Shape Our View of
terror*, Edward S Herman and Gerry
O'Sullivan (New York: Pantheon
Books, 1989)
The Terrorism Reader, David J Whittaker,
Editor (London: Routledge, 2001)
*Terrorism Versus Democracy: The Liberal
State Response*, Paul Wilkinson
(London: Frank Cass, 2001)
The Ultimate Terrorists, Jessica Stern
(Cambridge, MA: Harvard University
Press, 1999)
Unholy War: Terror in the Name of Islam,
John L Esposito (New York: Oxford
University Press, 2002)
Violence, Terrorism, and Justice, edited
by RG Frey (Cambridge New York:
Cambridge University Press, 1991)

Index